Endorsements

"I have known Heather and Adonis Lenzy for several years, including their courtship. They have written a wonderful book full of practical advice for singles, with marriage in mind. They are very transparent as they share their own failures and victories in a balanced and wholesome approach to dating. This roadmap to building Christ-like relationships will actually benefit everyone. The wisdom in this book can prevent a world of hurt and direct you down a biblical path to love! Enjoy!"

JOAN HUNTER
Author/Evangelist
President Joan Hunter Ministries

"*Dating in Black and White* is fresh and inspiring. We love Heather and Adonis's open and transparent insight into their lives. It's great to see how they have applied and tested the truths of this book before sharing them with the reader. This book gives a good biblical and practical foundation to help singles live their lives in a God-pleasing way. We intend to make *Dating in Black and White* a required read for the entire singles ministry of our church."

DRS. BILL & ANNE MOORE
Livingway Family Church, Brownsville, TX

"Before you have a 'Happily Ever After,' you must have a successful 'Once Upon a Time.' Through their own story, Adonis and Heather share principles and action steps to build a relationship. Their transparency is refreshing, and their wisdom is solid. If you are experiences, this book is for you. There is Your 'Once Upon a Time' is closer than you think; it's all here in *black and white*."

PASTORS DANNY & JILLIAN CHAMBERS
Oasis Church, Nashville, TN

"Amazingly relevant! Adonis and Heather Lenzy hit the nail on the head with their transparent, contemporary, balanced, and "black and white" message on the subject of dating from a Biblical perspective. No matter your age or background, the principles presented in this book are an essential roadmap for dating in the twenty-first century. It's not only a great read for singles but also an essential addition to any pastor or leader's library!"

PASTOR AND AUTHOR, AARON DAVIS
(The Tattooed Preacher)

"Having attended Pastor Adonis and Heather's church for the past six years, I've had the opportunity to watch them model a beautiful, love-filled relationship. They are both extremely real people who've been through relational struggles and challenges, and yet they've learned from their mistakes and used the lessons to build a very successful marriage. In February of 2011, Pastor Adonis officiated my wedding ceremony, and his and Heather's relationship continues to be a wonderful inspiration for my own marriage. I'm excited to see them continue motivating others through this book!"

KRISTINA ELLIS
Best-Selling Author and Speaker

"Adonis and Heather Lenzy have taken an often challenging and confusing topic and provided fresh insights, wisdom, and practicality for dating relationships. It's not often that you'll find the combination in one book, but I believe their transparency and humor provide a roadmap for couples looking for a godly way to discover and pursue each other."

RANDY K. BLUE
COO and CFO, Oasis Church
Executive Coach and Consultant

DATING IN BLACK & WHITE

Keeping Relationships on Target

ADONIS & HEATHER LENZY

ISBN: 978-0-9829516-6-8

Published by Hunter Books
PO Box 411
Pinehurst, TX 77362 USA
www.joanhunter.org

Managing Editor: Alice Sullivan, alicesullivan.com
Cover Design: Troy Dossett, thumbprintcreative.com
Interior Design and Typeset: theDESKonline.com
Author Photo: Russ Harrington, russharrington.com
Book Web Page: Jeremy Binns, jeremybinns.com

CONTENTS

ACKNOWLEDGMENTS

God – Without Your love and strength, none of this would have been possible. Thank You for allowing our paths to cross in Nashville, TN. You have truly blessed our broken roads and given us a relationship with one another that we will cherish for the rest of our lives. Your amazing grace truly inspired and empowered us to share our story with the world.

Pastors Danny & Jillian Chambers – Thank you for your continued guidance and counsel throughout our dating process. We never thought our journey would eventually be shared with the world. Your wisdom was truly a tool that forged our relationship and laid a strong foundation for our marriage. We are not only honored to call you our Pastors, but you are truly our family.

Ted & Charity Bradshaw – Your friendship to the both of us is simply amazing. Your love and support has been a great encouragement through the many ups and downs along the way. Thanks for believing in us.

Joan Hunter – Your love and support was over the top. Your belief in us and in our abilities kept us going and was a continued force throughout this entire process. You truly treated us like a part of your family.

Alice Sullivan – Wow! We will never forget your words of advice when you told us to just sit down and start writing. Well that's exactly what we did and you beautifully laid out the words to our life in the manuscript. We are forever grateful to you for being our editor and our friend.

David Sams – Thank you for the suggestion on the book title and encouraging us to be transparent and relevant with our story.

Troy Dossett – Thanks so much for your patience in working with us and in designing the cover. All the emails finally paid off. You truly found what we were visualizing inside of us and brought it out for all to see.

David Sluka – We would have been lost without your guidance and help in making the finished product. We're so thankful that we connected and we are looking forward to many more projects with you.

Michelle Moore – Thank you so much for teaching the writing class at church that truly served as a catalyst for us to start writing. We're so thankful that you kept pushing us to write, write, write. Your voice was another confirmation that it was the right time.

Russ Harrington – Thank you for making us look like super stars. The photo shoot was an experience that we will never forget. You rock, dude.

INTRODUCTION

In a world where dating is discussed from many view points, angles, and opinions, it can be overwhelming at times. Singles are constantly being targeted by websites, ads, and dating experts, but not all of the information available about dating is helpful—or healthy.

We're not dating experts. We're also not a perfect couple—no such thing exists. We are simply two people who are passionate about having healthy relationships, especially when it comes to dating and marriage. We're sharing our dating experiences (the good, the bad, and the ugly) in the hopes of providing direction, insight, advice, and knowledge about what a healthy dating relationship looks like. Whether you are single, dating, or divorced—this book is designed for you.

Now, this isn't a quick guide to a successful relationship; nor is it a promise that you will find that special someone after you finish reading this book. Our hope is that you will be better prepared for dating and for navigating all the side roads, detours, and fast lanes that come with it—both spiritually and relationally.

Somehow, we have strayed far away from applying biblical principles to our relationships. Besides your relationship with God, your relationship with your spouse is the most important relationship you can have. It is important to get that relationship right but, in order to get that right, you have to be intentional about your dating. After all, who you date is who you marry.

In this book, we will look at basic foundational things that you can do in your relationship to set you up for a great future; like practicing sexual purity and being free from baggage. Not only will we look at those foundational things, but we'll also look at practical things, such as navigating conflict and making good first impressions, to get your dating life heading in the right direction.

We'll discuss some key things that set us up for success, not only in dating, but in our marriage as well. We also want you to know that you will probably be hearing some new information in regards to dating. Our goal is to be open and honest, and that means we'll be covering some topics that the church, in general, often overlooks.

Through our dating process, we realized our story could help others. Since several of our single friends and church members were constantly asking us for relationship and dating advice, we started teaching a class called "Dating God's Way." We were only expecting about ten people to show up for our first class. To our surprise, we packed a small room out with about sixty people that night. Instantly, we knew that we had stumbled upon a great need.

First, Heather and I would like to say that *Dating in Black and White* was not produced from our perfection—we're far from perfect—but rather the pain of past relationships, mistakes, and failures, individually, as well as our journeys apart and together, that brought us to a healthy and happy marriage.

We are two people from different backgrounds and with different stories who became one. We are so honored and blessed to be able to share our story with you.

WHERE'S DATING IN THE BIBLE?

With all the many books, websites, and resources available on dating, the Bible is often the last resort simply because it doesn't talk a lot about dating. Back then, the father would either promise his daughter into marriage or simply give her away into marriage. That was it—done deal. I'm sure many women would have liked to have a say in the matter, but the Bible doesn't really talk much about that, either.

Although the Bible doesn't give us examples of dating, it does give us direction on how to live our lives as pleasing to God. It also gives us warnings about the pitfalls we might encounter if we don't. With this book, we aim to use the principles of God's Word and very practical life applications to equip, educate, and empower those in the dating arena to stay on target in their relationships.

We quickly came to realize that the truth, even though it's

hard for some to imagine, is that many good, Christian singles are or have been in a relationship that involved premarital sex, compromising, living together, or the lowering of standards; which was leading them totally off target of what God has for their lives. Let me be perfectly clear: Mistakes don't make you a bad person. Many good Christians make relational mistakes. The purpose of this book is to talk about these things openly and address some issues that will shed some light in the arena of dating. We also hope to help you avoid some of the mistakes that many people make (us included), and point you to some healthy guidelines that can lead to a successful relationship.

Maybe you've been hurt in a relationship and you no longer trust others; you've even become closed off to those around you. Maybe you've hurt others in past relationships and you're ready to break the cycle of repeated failures. You may have been through a bad divorce and don't know if you'll ever recover from the disappointment or shame that has tried to plague your mind from the moment you left the courtroom. Our prayer is that as you continue reading the stories on these pages, you will find hope, joy, laughter, and even relief from a hurting heart. We pray that you will also gain knowledge, understanding, and wisdom for your current or future dating relationship.

A Little Prayer before Reading Further

Dear God, please open up my heart as I read the words on these pages. Help me to recognize the things I need to apply to my life and my dating relationships; and help me see any of my mindsets, behaviors, beliefs, or actions that could possibly be stopping me from having a successful Godly relationship. Amen

HOW IT ALL BEGAN:
OUR STORY

God, he can't be the one for me; he probably doesn't even like Country music."

Heather and I met almost six years ago at a church in Nashville, Tennessee. I was the assistant Pastor and Heather had just moved to town from Phoenix, Arizona. I had noticed her during our church services, but didn't want to walk up to her directly and ask her out. That would be awkward for both of us. I was hoping that sooner or later, some type of conversation between us would just magically happen.

When I started a golf life group at church, I was super excited to find out that she liked to play golf! I invited her to be a part of the life group and I would email her to let her know when and where the group was meeting, but she always had an excuse for why she couldn't make it. I wondered if she suspected my intentions.

Still, I was no quitter, and one day she showed up at the driving range. I was with about five guys from the church, hitting from the artificial turf mats. Then, all of a sudden, I looked up and saw this beautiful blonde walking in our direction. It was her, and boy did my heart start pounding.

She looked like a professional golfer—even her outfit color coordinated with her golf bag. The closer she got to us, the more my heart raced. I didn't know what to say and I didn't want the guys to know that I liked her. So, when she got to where we were, I went into "Pastoral" mode.

The first thing I said to her was, "Praise the Lord, my sister! It's so good to see you here today."

Then she looked at where we were hitting and said, "I don't like to hit off the artificial mats so I'm going to walk way over there (pointing to the opposite end of the driving range) and hit from the grass."

I panicked because I thought I wasn't going to get to talk to her. I tried to convince her, in my "Pastoral" language, that it was important for us to stay as a group since this was our life group. She insisted that she was going to walk over to the grass area, and off she went. I made one of the best

Best Topics of Conversation on a First Date

Let's use wisdom here, gentlemen. If you love sports and she's not into sports, then it's probably not a great conversation topic. Ladies, if you love designer clothes and baking, and he's not into designer clothes or baking, then it's probably not a great conversation topic. Ask questions to find out what you have in common, such as:
- *Hobbies/Interests*
- *Travels*
- *Family*
- *Movies*
- *Food*

decisions of my life right then and there. I looked at the guys and said, "Grab your clubs, boys. We're going to the grass."

I tried to keep it as inconspicuous as I could, but didn't want that to be the last time we hung out together. So I said, "Hey, I noticed you have a good golf swing and you might just need a few pointers. I'd be more than happy to help you with that." She accepted the invitation and we met again at the driving range that weekend to work on her swing.

After our session, we went to a local restaurant to grab a bite to eat and that's when the conversation turned to music. Since then, she has told me she argued with God about going to hang out with me. She likes country music and it was important her future husband like it as well, and she just assumed I didn't like it. When she asked me what kind of music I listened to, I said, "I like listening to Motown, Keith Urban, Tim McGraw," (and a handful of others). You should have seen the look on her face!

From that moment on, our relationship began a journey that neither of us had been on before. As we look back now, we wouldn't trade our dating journey for anything. After being married for over five years and having two children, we are so thankful for the people who were with us, and for all the guidelines, guardrails, boundaries, and safeguards that were put in place as we walked this road together.

Adonis Has His Version of the Story; This Is Mine

Adonis approached me as I was walking out of church one day. He had heard I was a golfer and asked me if I would like to sign up for his golf life group. I thought it would be a great way for me to get out and enjoy something I like to do while meeting new people.

To be honest with you, I even thought there might be some single men in the group. You never know where you are going to meet someone! Little did I know that the person I was going to meet was going to be my pastor.

I wasn't able to make the first few meetings due to scheduling conflicts, and the next thing I knew, the life group semester was halfway through. I had been receiving the emails for the group meetings, but one day I received a text message from Adonis and decided I needed to go. After all, I hadn't been golfing in a long time and my schedule was actually free.

I showed up to the driving range and saw Adonis and a group of men hitting off the artificial turf mats. There was no way I was going to hit off those mats. They aren't like hitting off the grass, and the few times I had hit off the artificial mats, it didn't go so well.

It was a little bit awkward when Adonis greeted me. He was still in "Pastoral" mode, but it was different somehow. I let him know that I was going to head over to the grass area because I didn't want to hit off the mats. I knew it was a life group, but I wasn't about to make a fool of myself in front of all of these men. The next thing I know, all of the guys picked up their bags and followed me.

We talked while hitting and Adonis told me he'd be happy to help me with my swing. I didn't think much of it then, but looking back, that was a smooth move!

We met on the driving range a few times and, the next thing you know, we were grabbing a bite to eat in a Mexican restaurant. The rest is all history.

I was looking for a tall, dark, and handsome man who was a strong leader. I got exactly what I was looking for, but in an unexpected package—a handsome black preacher who likes country music! You have to love when God does that.

Adonis's Journey

My relationship journey has definitely been a long road filled with ups, downs, disappointments, and failures. For years, I couldn't figure out why I had such a hard time having a successful dating relationship. Even though I was a Christian, I still kept making very bad relational mistakes and choices that left me with regrets.

After a plethora of failed relationships, I finally realized that something was terribly wrong with me. I was a Christian and in church leadership, but was still unable to have a healthy dating relationship. That was such a horrible position to be in; it was like living a double life. I loved God and enjoyed what I did, but for some reason, I couldn't manage the relational part of my life successfully.

It wasn't until I met Heather that I finally pinpointed the experience, years earlier in my life, that altered my perception. When that light bulb came on, everything changed.

One day, I was thinking about my relationship with Heather. Everything was going great but, for some reason, I still feared marrying her. I remember asking God what was wrong with me. We had done everything right in the relationship and there was still something blocking me from wanting to move forward. I didn't understand it. Then, all of a sudden, it hit me. Some would call it a revelation, an epiphany, or an awakening. For me, it was a moment of clarity.

My mind flashed back to an incident from my teenage years, when my parents were going through some marital hardships. Early one morning, my dad came home from the railroad while everyone but me was gone. He walked into my bedroom and sat down at the foot of my bed with his back toward me. He never looked at me, or said, "Good morning, Son," or asked how I was doing. In a low, tiresome, exhausted tone of voice, he simply said, "Son, whatever you do, don't ever get married and don't ever have children."

It took me years to get those words out of my mind.

That's a heavy message for a teenager to hear. What's worse is that we never had a father-son talk about girls, sex, or relationships: This one exasperated line was the only relationship advice my dad ever gave me.

Shortly after that, my parents went through a horrible divorce, my dad left my mom and the family, and he moved away.

As I look back now, I know that he was frustrated and needed a counselor to vent to instead of his teenage son. In some ways, he probably thought he was giving me some good, fatherly advice that would make my life happier than his.

I don't blame my dad for my relational mistakes; I take full responsibility for my own actions. But imagine how those words shaped my thought life when it came to relationships and the thought of having children. For years, I struggled with those words without really knowing it. I would always say I was never getting married, and that it was just going to be me and Jesus for the rest of my life.

Subconsciously, those words my dad spoke over me produced in me a negative mindset regarding relationships. From that moment on, I felt like any relationship, future marriage, or having children had the potential to make me miserable. This produced a string of failed relationships in my life for several reasons.

For one, I had a low level of commitment since I knew I didn't want to get married. Second, those words from my dad were like a curse that plagued my relationships and kept me from having true feelings. I wanted to be with a woman, but wasn't willing to commit to one.

As much as it pains me to say, I didn't know how to have a Godly dating relationship that could possibly lead to marriage. I was a Christian. I loved God and knew His Word. Yet, some relationships went outside of His Word and crossed over into pre-marital sex. I was torn, confused, hurting, and in bondage, and didn't know how to escape. The guilt and shame were so heavy; it was like carrying the weight of the world on my shoulders. What if others found out I was a failure in relationships? I'm supposed to be a good example! Why couldn't I do this right? It was like a hidden force that sabotaged any relationship I had from that point forward.

I have made many relational mistakes along my journey. Mistakes that I am not proud of. Mistakes that left others hurt and wounded. Mistakes that I pray others can avoid by reading our story. But, when I had that epiphany, imagining myself sitting in my room as my dad spoke those hurtful words over me, I realized that I had a choice to make. His words were not true. The lies I had believed about relationships could be reversed. I could choose to move forward into a healthy and happy future. When I made that choice, the fears vanished.

Heather's Journey

One of the hardest struggles in my life has been my relationships with men. I struggled partly because I didn't have God or a model

21

of a healthy relationship at home. I also struggled with relationships because I wanted to do whatever I pleased.

Growing up, my parents had more of a friendship than a marriage. They lived very separate lives, each doing what they enjoyed doing, without each other.

We lived on a farm and, after he finished his 9-to-5 job, my dad was usually out farming the land. My mom was a hair stylist with a salon in our basement. In our free time, she and I would go shopping while my dad and brother stayed at home and worked in the garage or on the farm. We would sometimes go camping as a family, but my dad would stay out fishing all day and night, and my mom would stay at the campsite with us. Rarely would my parents do anything as a couple.

The reality is that my parents had a loveless marriage. It may not have started off that way, but somewhere along the way they became more like roommates than spouses. They spent so little time together, I'm not even sure they were friends. They finally divorced when I was twenty-one, but my views on relationships and marriage had long been set by then.

I had my first boyfriend when I was just fifteen years old. We dated for two years and when that fizzled, I was single for a few months before I found someone else. When I dated someone, it was fun and exciting in the beginning. But once the excitement was gone, I was done with the relationship. I had developed a dating pattern: Excitement, fizzle, excitement, fizzle.

I even continued this pattern into my first marriage. Somehow, I thought marriage was going to be different and end the pattern I had created. It was exciting at first, then fizzled and ended in divorce. I knew there had to be a different way, but I had no idea how to get there. I didn't want to be a long-term dater forever. I also knew one day I wanted to have children. But how was I going to have children with someone when I couldn't even like them for more than two years?

I finally started to ask myself, "What am I doing wrong?" I began praying and asking God to show me what I needed to do. That's when I finally met God and decided that I was going to start living my life differently. I might as well try His way; mine never seemed to work out.

I moved to Nashville and started attending Oasis Church in October of 2006. Six months after that, God placed me in the home of a Christian couple, where I really saw what marriage should look like. The more I saw, the more I desired to have the same thing myself. I was in that home when I met Adonis.

But let me take you back a little bit.

I married when I was in my mid-twenties. I thought I couldn't have picked a nicer man. We had a lot in common: We were both career-minded, enjoyed sports, music, and hanging out with friends, and we both wanted a family someday.

We purchased a house together before we were married. I thought I had met my perfect match and it was supposed to be a fairy-tale ending. So where did it go wrong?

The problem was that we were more friends than husband and wife. Sure, we loved each other, but love doesn't automatically give you passion. As I said earlier, there was passion in the beginning of our relationship, but it fizzled even before we got married. I should have recognized that as a red flag, but I didn't.

Even though it followed the same pattern as my other relationships, I loved him more than anyone in my past and I was convinced no one else was more suited for me. Still, as it fizzled, instead of dealing with the same problem again, I started to hang out at the bars more with my friends and take trips to Vegas and music festivals. At some point, I became completely disengaged from my marriage. We tried counseling, which was mostly a formality because I didn't believe things would change. I still loved him very much, but I had convinced myself we were only friends. After two years of marriage, we divorced and I felt like a failure.

I knew I needed to make some changes so I began to live my life differently, but the people around me weren't. They still wanted to go out to the bars and clubs, and I didn't have the courage or will to say no. Still, I knew I could no longer live with one foot in God and one foot in the world. So, I accepted a job in Nashville and I left my old life behind in Phoenix.

Now I was alone in a new city with a six-month lease on an apartment. It was literally me and God. It was then that God began to peel back layer after layer and started to show me areas where my heart needed to change. I checked out other churches in the area, but Oasis Church was the first church I attended in Nashville and that's where I stayed.

When my lease was up, I was going to move in with a roommate but it fell through at the last minute. In a desperate attempt to find a place to live, I called a friend I'd met at church. I asked if she knew of anyone looking for a roommate and, a few minutes later, I received a call from her sister, Charity. Charity, whom I had actually just met a few days before, said that she and her husband, Ted, had a room available for me to rent in their home, and both Roxy (my big dog) and I were welcome. I would have never chosen to move in with a couple and their two-year-old, but God knew that's where I needed to be and He closed the door to all other possibilities.

That one move set a series of events into motion. I moved in with Ted and Charity in April of 2007. I saw first-hand what a good Christian marriage looks like, and what raising a child in a Christian home looks like. Adonis and Ted were friends, and I began attending Adonis's life group the very next month. Ted and Charity even became our accountability partners when Adonis and I began dating several months later.

Manners for Guys

- Open the door.
- Treat her like a lady because she is one.
- Don't chew with your mouth open.
- Don't lick the food off of your fingers (unless you are eating BBQ, in which case, keep the smacking sound at a minimum).
- Treat her, and others, with kindness.
- Say, "Thank you" and "I appreciate that."
- Don't be loud and obnoxious.
- Hold your hand out for her if she is walking on stairs or getting out of the car.
- Don't interrupt when she's talking.
- Put your phone away: No texting while talking.

Manners for Girls

- Say, "Please" and "Thank you."
- Don't be loud and obnoxious.
- Don't make jokes at his expense.
- Give him your undivided attention.
- Don't come across too uppity.
- Take his hand or arm if he offers it while walking on stairs or getting out of the car.
- Don't interrupt him when he's talking.
- Put your phone away: No texting while talking.

NEVER DATE ALONE:

Why You Need Spiritual Authority and Accountability

L et's face it: Dating can be one of the most adventurous things you ever do. You're hanging out with someone you like and who, hopefully, likes you in return. You begin to talk about the future and what it would feel and look like. It's fun, exciting, and can send you on an emotional high for days. The problem is that when you are so caught up in the emotional high, you can no longer see the caution signs or deal-breakers that have come up in your dating journey.

A spiritual authority who will act as your accountability partner can help you see the danger when you are too "in love" to see it, and they can see the good when you're too scared to admit it, too. When there is no accountability, there's a greater chance for relational failure that can leave your emotions damaged, your heart broken, and your spirit crushed.

By the time, I (Adonis) started dating in my teenage years, my parents had divorced and my dad had left us for good. Like I said, I never had man-to-man talks with him about dating do's and don'ts. I never reached out to my mother, siblings, or friends about my relationships, either. By default, I just depended on myself to navigate through any emotions and hardships; it was a part of me that I kept to myself.

This behavior followed me into my adult years and relationships as well. I never sought counsel or asked anyone for advice or opinions. Even worse than that, if someone gave me a non-favorable opinion, I would get defensive, which would, in turn, reaffirm my habit of not letting others into my personal life.

Having accountability is a must, in our opinion, if you are going to date in a healthy way. Now, remember that in order for this to be effective, you will need to do two things correctly: You will need to find the right accountability partner or partners, and you will need to be honest with them *at all times*. If you have to lie to your accountability partner about your relationship, that's a good indicator that your relationship has gone out of bounds in some area and you're feeling the need to hide it.

Choosing Your Spiritual Authority

It's very important that you choose your spiritual authority wisely. It needs to be someone who has the same beliefs as you, loves you, and wants the best for you, but it also needs to be someone who can be honest with you. It has to be someone you can receive from and submit to, even when you don't like what they have to say.

Your spiritual authority needs to be someone you can go to when you're having struggles in your relationship, and that can help you through those struggles. It's probably not a good idea for your spiritual authority to be someone who hasn't had a successful relationship or someone who is still carrying around baggage from past relationships.

If you are having struggles, then you have to be honest with your spiritual authority about those struggles and reveal the *entire* truth to them. Keep in mind that if you can't give your spiritual authority all the details or the entire truth, then I think you already know the answer to your situation. Since you could potentially be revealing the good, the bad, and the ugly about yourself and the person you are dating, you probably don't want your spiritual authority to be a family member or your best friend. Parents will be inclined to look out for the best interest, in their opinion, of their child, and a best friend might have a hard time telling you something you don't want to hear.

One of the best pieces of advice I ever got before I got married was that when you fight with your spouse, never go to your family members. You love your spouse and will eventually forgive and forget. Your family, however, does not have that same love toward your spouse. Family may forgive, but they will never forget...and that can make Thanksgiving dinner very awkward! That same advice is applicable here. Your spiritual authority should be the person celebrating your relationship the most. If your spiritual authority isn't celebrating your relationship with you, then Houston, we have a problem!

- Ask yourself, "Who is my authority?" and, "Am I submitting to them?" If not, study God's Word and ask Him to help you to submit.

- Choose your spiritual authority and make sure it's someone that you know has God's best interest for you at heart. It's not too late to do this even if you're already dating someone. It's not too early, either; don't wait until you start dating to find your spiritual authority.
- Recognize other couples that are successful in their marriage or relationship and spend time with them.

This is crucial in your dating relationship. Both you and your significant other must each choose someone you are personally comfortable with and willing to give access to speak freely into your relationship without you getting defensive.

You can each have your own accountability partner or you can have one together. If you choose to share an accountability partner, then it's wise to choose someone neutral. You don't want to leave room for anyone to be biased in their counsel or advice.

Examples of Good Accountability Partners

- Pastors
- Christian leaders
- Someone who has a successful marriage
- Someone who is committed to seeing God's will done in your life
- Someone who has your best interest at heart

Examples of Questionable Accountability Partners

1. Someone who has had one failed relationship after the other

Just because they have a lot of relationship experience, it doesn't automatically qualify them to speak into your dating relationship and offer you wise counsel.

2. Someone who still carries baggage from past relationships

You will be amazed at how many people still carry baggage from prior relationships. If they are still wounded and hurt from a past relationship, then it will become very evident in their counsel to you. For example, you may go to them with a small issue in your relationship that is similar to something they went through in one of their last failed relationships. If they still haven't gotten over it, your current issue will only bring up their past issue and their advice will be filtered through their hurt, emotions, and baggage that they are still carrying around.

3. Your best friends

They may have a tendency to be biased toward you because of your friendship. They may also be hesitant to tell you the truth if they think it could jeopardize the friendship.

4. A family member

I'm not saying that family members don't care for you or want the best for you. What I want you to be aware of is that, chances are, you will share both the good and bad experiences about your dating journey with your accountability partner. For example, let's say you get hurt by the person you are dating and you share your experience with one of your family members.

Being hurt or getting upset or disappointed in a relationship is normal. It happens and it doesn't mean that you aren't meant for each other, but it does allow you to see how you both will process it, deal with it, and bring a resolution. If it's fixable, you can prove that by the both of you walking through the process of forgiving, apologizing, putting it behind you, and moving forward.

The only problem is that you have forgiven them and moved on, but your family member hasn't and that makes any future family gatherings awkward. Nobody can hold a grudge like family, so be careful how much you share with them.

The Benefits of Dating with Spiritual Authority

"Have confidence in your leaders and submit to their authority, because they keep watch over you as those who must give an account. Do this so that their work will be a joy, not a burden, for that would be of no benefit to you…" (Hebrews 13:17 NIV)

As adults, we too often think, "I'm grown and I don't need anyone to coach me along in a relationship." Submitting to authority doesn't mean you've given up control, but it does mean you are letting someone help guide you along the way. The Bible clearly teaches us to follow the counsel of those in authority. To us, not dating alone meant having others involved in our dating process.

When my wife and I were dating, this was a huge step for both of us, and for very different reasons. I had been an associate pastor for several years and understood what it meant to submit to authority. However, it was still hard for me to let other people get involved with my personal life. I felt like I needed at least one area in my life that I could have all to myself without anyone butting in—my dating relationships. As it turned out, that was a huge mistake on my part.

Heather, on the other hand, did not grow up in ministry or church, so submission was very new to her. As a strong-willed and independent woman, in the beginning of our relationship she really struggled with the idea of submission in general.

Now, our experience is not the norm for every dating relationship. Keep in mind, I was an associate pastor of a large church, and Heather, at the time, was very new to ministry. When we knew that we had feelings for each other and wanted to get to know each other better, I knew I was going to have to involve our church leaders. This was very hard for the both of us; not because we don't have great leaders, but because I was uncomfortable sharing details about my personal life and Heather felt like she had to go through extra steps just to date me.

When we met with our pastors, who we had chosen to be our spiritual authority, they instructed us to double date with the core leaders of the church—eight different couples. Now, as I mentioned earlier, our situation was very different since I was a pastor in a large church. Our pastors' wisdom, advice, and instruction were both for our protection and the protection of our ministry and the church. They asked us not to have any physical contact with each other, which meant no kissing and no holding hands. They also asked us not to announce to anyone that we were dating other than our family, close friends, and church leaders.

As we look back on what we thought were strange requests, we are so thankful, because they kept us from crossing physical lines in our relationship and helped us get to know each other better. Oh yes, even Christians can cross those lines. I've been there, done that, and didn't want to do it again.

It also allowed us to have a relationship without dealing with the opinions of others in the process. (We'll talk more about this in a later chapter.) Once again, we know this is not the norm for every dating relationship, but we both feel that these guidelines are what produced a great dating relationship, which eventually led to a healthy, loving marriage. We are not stating that this is the only way to date, but we definitely recognize what it did for us. We truly believe that the principles we learned and the way we dated can be adopted in some degree by any dating couple that is willing to pursue a healthy, godly relationship.

Double Date with Other Couples You Admire

Not only is it important to have spiritual authority in your life while dating, but it's also important that you go on dates with other couples. And not just any couples. Be selective and choose couples that have a successful relationship or a successful marriage.

R-E-S-P-E-C-T Good for You and Good for Me

A dating relationship should be a relationship in which both people honor and respect each other privately and publicly. When Heather and I were dating, we made sure that no matter what we were going through, we would never share anything negative about the other outside of the two of us and our accountability partners. We both knew that upholding and encouraging your partner shows them great honor and respect. We also made it a point to never belittle each other in front of family or friends, whether in an angry way or even in a joking manner. If we had issues or quarrels, we would always work them out privately.

Fighting or arguing in public will only cause those around you to think very negatively about your relationship. It will create a perception that will leave a lasting impression. You will be forever labeled the fighting couple and it will do major damage to your relationship.

I (Adonis) can honestly say that our dating relationship was the first time I ever let someone else in to be a part of the journey. All my past relationships were very isolated and without accountability, and therefore ended up failing and going in the wrong direction. Now I had direction, encouragement, and people who truly wanted to help us succeed in our relationship.

Dating One-on-One: Moving to the Next Level

The first time I ever heard the words "Don't date alone," I was a teenager in my youth group at church. Then I thought it was a way for church leadership to keep us teenagers out of trouble. As I look back now, I think it is a safe way to prevent dating couples from ending up in the wrong place at the wrong time, and from doing something that they would both regret. It also seems like a good way to prevent dating couples from having premarital sex.

I am not knocking this approach at all. I think dating in groups works just fine when you're a teenager just starting out in the whole dating arena. I'm pretty sure my daughter will hear that from me when she's old enough to date. But the older you get, you need to start being responsible for your actions and the welfare of your relationships. If you are thirteen, dating in a group is about all you can handle. If you are thirty, then it's time to grow up and be mature enough in your decision-making when it comes to dating.

Heather and I have chosen to go beyond that safe "Christianese" answer and give dating couples real advice. We want to show them that going out to dinner, a movie, or dancing is still possible without ending up in the wrong place at the wrong time, doing something you'll regret. We want to be able to equip dating couples with boundaries and guardrails that can ensure success in their dating. To us, success in a relationship is not dependent upon whether or not you end up getting married. Rather, success in a relationship is determined by your emotional, spiritual, and mental health, regardless of whether you stay together or not.

We have to give dating couples the pros and cons of dating in the right places versus dating in the wrong places. For example, if you are a dating couple, it might eliminate any temptation when deciding whether to go to a movie theatre to watch a movie versus staying at home to watch a movie on the sofa all by yourselves. Think about it. Both places are dark and cozy but the theatre provides a level of accountability that your sofa doesn't provide.

There are also numerous benefits that Heather and I experienced by dating in groups. In addition to being in a safe environment, we were able to see how the other person interacted with friends and how we would interact together around people.

This was great in the beginning, but as our relationship progressed, we needed time alone to really get to know each other. We noticed that being out in a group didn't allow us the one-on-one time that we needed.

Here is where you may find a difference of opinions in the church arena. Nowhere in the Bible does it tell you where you can and can't go on a date. I believe it's up to the couple to be responsible to not put themselves in a position that can potentially lead to a weak moment.

Heather and I discussed some options because we really wanted to spend some time alone but didn't want to put ourselves in a tempting situation. We were both adults and made a huge commitment to keep sexual purity in our relationship. We were very physically attracted to each other as well. It's not that we were afraid that we wouldn't be able to uphold the commitment, but we were also aware that by this time we were very emotionally attached and felt like there was a huge potential for us to be married one day.

Make no mistake about it. Physical attraction is a very strong force that has to be managed in a dating relationship and that's exactly what we did. I can't tell you how many times I've heard a dating couple say, "We don't how that happened," or "We never thought we would end up crossing that line but we did." Heather and I knew that it was better to be safe than sorry. When the time came for us to go out alone, we chose places and activities that would foster our commitment to sexual purity with one another.

Now, I know that every dating relationship is different and if you've set goals for your relationship in the area of sexual purity, then you have to manage that on your own. Figure out what kind of dating activities you can do together that would keep you safely within the boundaries of your commitment.

Boundaries are your friend. Regard them and thrive, disregard them and your relationship will take a dive.

10 Fun Things to Do on a First Date

1. Have a picnic in the park. (Each of you can agree to make something homemade or go for store-bought.)

2. Go out to one of your favorite restaurants. (Unless your favorite restaurant is Waffle House.)

3. Go to a sporting event. (That is, if you both like sports.)

4. Meet for coffee. (Caffeine gives some the gift of gab, so be careful with this one.)

5. Go to a comedy show. (It's easier to have a good time when you are laughing.)

6. Play a round of miniature golf or take a spin on the go-carts. (You'll learn if they are competitive really quickly.)

7. Go bowling. (Be selective on your attire; you don't want to find out what happens when your pants are too tight.)

8. Go to a museum. (This gives you more things to talk about and if it doesn't work out, at least you learned something.)

9. Go to a cooking class. (Dinner and entertainment is covered.)

10. Go to a local tourist trap. (Pretend you are tourists and check out things in your city you've avoided.)

ROLES IN RELATIONSHIPS: WHAT SUBMITTING REALLY MEANS

Ah, we've arrived at the topic of submission. I know you're probably thinking, "Why are they talking about submitting in a dating book?" The answer is quite simple: If you are in a dating relationship that is headed toward marriage, then you better make sure you are well aware of the roles and responsibilities that both of you will have.

The Bible talks about it, but what does it mean to be submissive? Most people have a negative connotation of that word because they see it as a dictatorship. I (Heather) can speak from the women's perspective here. We tend to feel that submission is a role of being dominated over or being lesser than, because the Bible says that wives are supposed to submit to their husbands.

Some women get a mental image of a selfish, uncaring husband who will order her around. She fears she will lose her individuality and her voice, and become nothing more than property. Now, that's an extreme interpretation of this verse, but I'd be willing to bet that a lot of women roll their eyes at the word "submission" precisely because of these assumptions.

What we forget to look at (and what some men forget as well) is the following line of scripture that says husbands are to love their wives as Christ loves the church.

Let's take a look at Ephesians 5:22–28 (MSG):

Wives, understand and support your husbands in ways that show your support for Christ. The husband provides leadership to his wife the way Christ does to his church, not by domineering but by cherishing. So just as the church submits to Christ as he exercises such leadership, wives should likewise submit to their husbands.

Husbands, go all out in your love for your wives, exactly as Christ did for the church—a love marked by giving, not getting. Christ's love makes the church whole. His words evoke her beauty. Everything he does and says is designed to bring the best out of her, dressing her in dazzling white silk, radiant with holiness. And that is how husbands ought to love their wives. They're really doing themselves a favor—since they're already "one" in marriage.

It's easy to submit to a man who loves their wife as Christ loves the church. It's not so easy to submit to a man who leads in a controlling, rather than a loving, way. If you marry a man who will lovingly lead you, he's easy to follow. And, as I've said before, you will eventually marry someone you date. Dating is practice for marriage.

So what does submission mean? And what *doesn't* it mean?

Men, submission isn't where you say, "I run the household," or "I make the decisions." It's where you lead in a loving way. She needs to know that she is loved; that you care for her more than you care for yourself and that you are making choices for you both based on a love for her, not selfishness.

For example, when Adonis and I were dating, we hit a few bumps in the road. In fact, our first major bump threatened to break us. It was in that moment that Adonis grabbed my hand and prayed, "Lord, if we aren't for each other, please reveal that to us and help us to part ways. If we are for each other, please change our hearts and help us work this out." That was a very selfless prayer. He put his feelings aside and prayed for God to work it out either way, even if that meant we would go our separate ways. I knew from that moment on that Adonis was a selfless man who I could trust, and who could lead in a loving, not a controlling, way.

Women and Submission

Many women say they are looking for a strong Christian man, one that can lead them. That can be intimating to men. Am I right, men? Not all men have a take-charge personality. Some men have a more passive personality, but that doesn't mean that they can't lead a household. A soft-spoken man can be a leader. He may not be on the stage on a Sunday morning preaching a message, but he can certainly pray and lead by example.

Women, we can scare off men by saying we are looking for a

strong man to lead us; in reality, we are looking for a man who has a relationship with God and is following God.

Take our friends, for example: The wife has a strong personality and her husband does not. You would think that she "wears the pants in the family," but she doesn't. Even though she has a strong personality, she is able to submit to her husband. Without a doubt, she knows that he loves her and that he will guard and protect her. And just because she submits to her husband, that doesn't change her personality. She can still have her strong personality and, yet, submit to him.

Having a strong personality does not give women the excuse to say, "This is how God made me. Deal with it." The fact is that God made us to submit to our husbands, whether we're housewives or the big bosses at work; and He has called men to love and respect their wives or girlfriends while in a dating relationship. The minute one person isn't feeling the love or starts putting demands on the other, that's when the word submission turns into a negative thing.

Men and Submission

We've talked about women submitting to their husbands, but the Bible also talks about men submitting to leaders, and to God and His Word. Hebrews 13:17 (NIV) says, "Have confidence in your leaders and submit to their authority, because they keep watch over you as those who must give an account. Do this so that their work will be a joy, not a burden, for that would be of no benefit to you." Everyone needs to submit to authority.

Who is your authority? If you're a teenager living at home, then your parents are your authority. If you work for someone, then your boss is your authority.

How does the person you are dating, or potentially want to date, submit to authority? You can learn a lot about someone's respect for authority by the way they talk.

Although you aren't there to witness their interactions, if they bash their boss, that is a good indication that they aren't submitting to their authority.

In the workplace especially, we don't always have the same opinions as our bosses. We aren't going to necessarily agree with every decision they make or everything they say. Regardless, our boss has been placed in a position of authority and we are called to submit to their authority.

How does the person you are dating, or potentially want to date, submit to their pastors? The same thing applies here; do they complain or bash their pastors or leaders in the church?

You're probably asking yourself, "What does submitting to my boss or pastors have to do with dating?" A lot, actually.

Women, if you are dating someone who doesn't submit to his boss, pastors, or parents, then there is a good chance he has some issues with authority figures.

Men, if you are dating someone who doesn't submit to her boss, pastors, or parents, then she probably isn't going to submit to you.

When Adonis and I were dating, we were truly challenged by submitting to our authority, but came out on the other side with so much knowledge as a result of that experience.

Finances and Submission

The topic of finances was a tough one for us. While we were dating, we talked about finances and what that would look like for us in a future marriage. We decided that it would be best to have Adonis in charge of our finances because he was more detailed than I was and he had just gone through Dave Ramsey's *Financial Peace*.

I'd controlled my finances my entire adult life. I made the money; it was my money and I could spend it however I wanted. I thought, "I'm not going to just give up my money to someone!" But I had to learn that once we married, it was no longer mine, but ours. It didn't matter if I made more money or I made less money. Our money was going to be our money.

Submitting to Spiritual Authority

Now as you recall, when Adonis and I decided to start dating, we met with our pastors—our authority. Adonis met with Pastor Danny alone and I met with Pastor Jill alone. I will never forget my meeting with her. She said she would like us to go on dates with the leaders in the church. Then she asked that Adonis and I refrain from any physical contact—she specifically said no kissing, hugging, or even handholding. I left her office thinking, "What have I gotten myself into? I'm a thirty-something-year-old woman and I have to go on dates with a bunch of people I don't know and can't hold Adonis's hand or kiss him?" Needless to say, I had a really bad attitude when I left there. Then the Lord reminded me that I wanted a right relationship.

Pastor Jill didn't ask me to follow these guidelines in order to punish me or deny me anything; it was for my protection. That is the purpose of having spiritual authority. You first have to seek guidance from someone whom you place in that position, and then you have to follow through. Had I not done what Pastor Jill had asked of me then, I wouldn't have learned the lessons I learned.

How Does Submitting Play Out in a Dating Relationship?

Submitting to one another in a dating relationship falls under the category of honoring and respecting one another's wishes and expectations. It's not forced, as in "I have to do this." It's more respectful, as in "I get to show the person I'm in a relationship with that I care about what matters to them." Those are two completely different approaches.

When Heather and I were dating, we each wanted to make sure that we were respecting each other in the process. Early on in our relationship, Heather was going to have lunch with a guy friend of hers who she'd known for years and was in town for a few days. She invited me to go along but I already had a previous commitment that I couldn't change.

Heather went without me and the whole night the thought of the girl I was dating being out with another guy bothered me, even though they were only friends. And Heather was feeling the same way. After that night, she told me it didn't feel right to be out with another man without me there, even though they had a friendship. So, we both made an agreement to never be out alone with anyone of the opposite sex regardless of the occasion. This is something we both submitted to and continue to honor to this day.

Let's look at this from a practical point of view. One of the definitions for the word submission is to defer to another's judgment, opinion, or decision. Here are a few examples of how this can be played out in a dating relationship:

1. Guys, let her choose the movie and then act excited about it even though it's a chick flick and you hate chick flicks. You're spending time with her.

2. Ladies, let him decide where to go for dinner and act excited even though there is nothing on the menu that excites you. You're spending time with him.

3. Instead of you always picking the weekend activities, let the other person choose.

DEAL-BREAKERS, COMPROMISES, AND RED FLAGS

I t is important to establish deal-breakers in your dating relationships. These are set in place to keep you from moving forward in your relationship if there is an issue that would eventually make you miserable in the future and could potentially ruin a marriage. It's also important to know which areas or issues you can compromise without resentment.

A lot of people misunderstand what deal-breakers are and how they are meant to help you—not harm you. A deal-breaker is something you establish as an *individual* before you get too emotionally connected to someone you're dating—before you're head-over-heels in love. All too often, people get involved so quickly they forget to pay attention to the signs and issues—red flags—that could potentially destroy the relationship. Or worse—they see them but ignore them altogether.

A deal-breaker is *black and white*; it leaves no room for compromise. It is the one thing (or multiple things) that you will not allow into your relationship. Deal-breakers can consist of both spiritual and practical matters, and they must be established while you are in a sober state of mind, *before* you become too emotionally connected to another person.

Those who have a tendency to ignore deal-breakers have what we call "emotional blinders." They are willing to compromise in an area that has the potential to ruin something in their future. This is also another good reason to have accountability partners while dating; they're not prone to the emotional blinders that you are.

Deal-Breakers

Besides the core foundational issues (dating a believer, sexual purity, submitting to authority, and being free from baggage), it's important to determine what your deal-breakers are, as your deal-breakers are going to be unique to you.

You also need to know that if you encounter a deal-breaker, you have the strength to walk away from the relationship and not settle. Don't let the fear of never finding someone cause you to settle for the wrong one.

Yes, it can be an upsetting and difficult choice to make, but you will be much happier in the long-run when you can stand up for yourself.

If you are single, take some time right now and list the things that are very important to you—things that you will not compromise in a relationship. If you are already dating someone, evaluate your relationship and make sure you aren't making allowances for any deal-breakers.

In my case (Heather), my date not liking country music really was a deal-breaker for me. I know that sounds like a funny deal-breaker, but I listen to music a lot! It's a good thing Adonis blazed through that one. However, we ran into a few more obstacles.

Figure out what your deal-breakers are, but also determine if they're realistic. You also need to identify them long before you enter into marriage.

Let's say you don't want to have children. You meet someone wonderful; they're everything you've been looking for, but they want at least four children. That means if you don't want any children and they want four, the compromise could be two. You have to ask yourself if you really want two children. If not, then that's a major deal-breaker and you shouldn't continue in the relationship. If you are the other person, ask yourself if two children are enough and if they aren't, that's a major deal-breaker and you shouldn't continue in the relationship.

Another deal-breaker for me was whether the person I dated was clean or not. I knew I didn't want to spend every day of my life picking up after someone. That would cause strife and strain in my relationship, and that relationship would not last. Thankfully, Adonis keeps a clean house. Believe me, I made sure!

Once you create your list of deal-breakers, ask yourself why you have chosen those specific deal-breakers. Are they from past experiences and past hurts? Is it because you know yourself and what you can and can't handle? It's important to know why you have your deal-breakers, because they may be challenged at some point and if you don't have a plan, it's easy to compromise. Once you set your deal-breakers, discuss them with your spiritual authority and have them help hold you accountable for your deal-breakers once you start dating someone. Deal-breakers aren't set in stone because God can certainly change your heart, but they are a good indicator of whether or not you are compromising.

Compromises

When Heather and I were dating, she was very attached to her dog; it even slept on her bed. I had a dog when I was young and my dog lived outside in the doghouse we built for it. I wasn't accustomed to pets living indoors with me and I knew I would have to face this sooner or later if I continued my relationship with Heather. I know it seems like a little issue but, as I mentioned earlier, the little things have potential to cause big trouble. "The little foxes that spoil the vineyards [of our love] . . ." (Song of Solomon 2:15 AMP).

When we started talking about marriage, I had to decide what would be the compromise in this situation and what would be the deal-breaker. I knew that I could not spend the rest of my life waking up covered in dog hair. But I also knew she loved her dog. Long story short, we got married and the dog lived indoors with us but stopped at the bedroom door and Heather was okay with that.

This brings me to my next point. It's so important for you as an individual to be honest with the person you are dating if and when they discuss a deal-breaker with you. If you agree to something just because you fear loosing them, then you have just doomed that relationship for potential failure. So many people will put up with anything, including wrong behavior and habits, just to keep someone. Remember, what you put up with is what you end up with.

It's harder to break away once you are emotionally involved.

Take note, I said it's *harder*—not impossible. Even if you have a wedding date already set, it's not too late to yield to the deal-breakers.

Red- and Yellow-Flag Examples

Here are some red flag statements or beliefs:

- "I don't know whether or not I believe in God."
- "I don't take orders from anyone."
- "I hate my ex."
- "I think it's healthy to have many sexual partners."

Here are some yellow flag statements or beliefs:

- "I was raised in a religious home." (Someone can grow up going to church every Sunday and not know God; or their parents may have a relationship with God, but they don't.)
- "I don't always agree with my authority."
- "I have some financial issues."
- "It's okay to have sex if you are going to marry the person."

Red Flags

A red flag is different from a deal-breaker. A deal-breaker is something that you choose for yourself; beliefs or ideas that you want to hold firm to and not settle. A red flag is just like a red stoplight or stop sign—no matter what, you don't blow through it or there's a good chance you'll get hit.

Just like you don't ignore these red signals, you shouldn't ignore red flags while you are dating. You shouldn't ignore yellow flags, either. They mean that you may need to slow down and proceed with caution.

Sometimes, as Christians, we pray so long for our future spouse that we think the next person who walks into our lives is "The One." That's when we start to make allowances and blow through the red flags.

Your spiritual authority may come in handy here to help you see the red flags and work through the yellow flags. Keep in mind that you need to be honest with your spiritual authority for them to be able to help you. Just remember a red flag is a red flag; sugar coating it won't make it a green flag!

True Stories: Different Views on Premarital Sex

I (Heather) was counseling a friend of mine in her new relationship. Up to this point, things were going great. Then, one day, she called me in a panic. She and her boyfriend had a talk about premarital sex and he believed it was okay. She believed she should wait, so she didn't know how to continue the conversation.

I reminded her that not everyone was exposed to God's Word, the wisdom, or even the experience that she had been exposed to in this area. I told her to sit down and have a conversation with him about *why* she felt the way she did, instead of just giving her stance.

She called me back a few days later to tell me that after their talk, he had changed his views and that this no longer was an issue. He felt so compelled to learn about the reasons she felt so strongly that he even dug into God's Word and started telling her that "the moment wasn't worth a lifetime."

What seemed like it could have been a red flag was actually a yellow flag. It's a good thing my friend worked through that yellow flag because they are now happily married.

Deal-Breaker or Down the Aisle?

Tom and Janet had been dating for several months and everything was going great. In fact, they were already planning the wedding.

They had done everything the right way so far including not having premarital sex and going through premarital counseling; they even had accountability partners. They'd worked through the normal challenges, disagreements, and cautions that come along with any dating relationship. Then, out of nowhere, a big deal-breaker suddenly presented itself to Janet. It's hard to pay attention to deal-breakers once your emotions are involved; it's even harder when a wedding date has been set.

This deal-breaker that should have ended the relationship without hesitation, but they were in love and wanted to work through the situation. At first, Janet tried to find a way to save the relationship. You can imagine how she must have felt; preparation and planning for the big day had already begun.

In moments like these, it becomes a battle in your mind. You know the right thing to do but you still try to make it work. Besides that, you don't want to be embarrassed, especially since you've already shared the news of your joyous engagement with everyone.

In the end, Janet stood on her beliefs and was led by her spirit and not her emotions. She knew standing her ground would cause her relationship to end. Still, she found peace in her decision, went through some heartache (which is normal), and now can clearly see that it was the right decision for her and Tom.

It's important for you to know what your deal-breakers are and to write them down as a reminder of what you are not willing to ignore in a relationship. Take a moment to write down some deal-breakers.

What are your deal-breakers?

1. _____
2. _____
3. _____
4. _____
5. _____

15 Questions to Ask to Get to Know Someone Better

1. What do you like to do for fun?
2. What do you like to do when you aren't working?
3. Do you like to travel? If so, where have you traveled?
4. Is there someplace you haven't traveled to that you would like to?
5. Do you have any siblings?
6. Are you parents still married? If so, how long have they been married?
7. What are your favorite childhood memories?
8. What was it like growing up in your house?
9. What type of movies do you like?
10. What is your favorite movie?
11. What is your favorite TV show?
12. What genre of music do you listen to?
13. Is there any type of music you don't like?
14. What is your favorite kind of food?
15. What was your favorite meal growing up?

DATING A BELIEVER
AND SHARING PRACTICAL
BELIEF SYSTEMS

"Do not be unequally yoked with unbelievers
[do not make mismated alliances with them or
come under a different yoke with them, inconsistent
with your faith]." (2 Corinthians 6:14 AMP)

When you are looking at a potential person to date, you need to investigate their belief system and make sure that it aligns with yours. When we started dating, it was important to each of us to make sure that the other person was a believer. We also wanted to make sure we had similar values and priorities.

Dating a Believer

The place to start is to look at whether or not you are a believer in God and whether or not the person you are dating or want to date is a believer. If you get this right, you are off to a great start.

If you get this wrong, you're going to be in for a bumpy ride.

The Bible specifically mentions this in 2 Corinthians 6:14 (New King James), "Do not be unequally yoked together with unbelievers. For what fellowship has righteousness with lawlessness? And what communion has light with darkness?" A marriage is the only relationship in which two people can become one. As I've said before, you will eventually marry someone you date, so it is important to get this right in the dating stage.

So, what does it mean to be unequally yoked, and where does that term come from anyway? A yoke is the wooden bar that joins two oxen together so they can pull the load equally. If one of the oxen is strong and the other is weak, they will struggle to pull the load, be at odds with one another, and may even end up pulling it in circles. The Message Bible says it this way: "Don't become partners with those who reject God. How can you make a partnership out of right and wrong? That's not partnership; that's war." Do you really want to be at war with someone you are dating? Or, worse yet, at war with someone you marry?

This Bible verse is a general message to all Christians, but let's apply it toward dating. A believer in Christ shouldn't date someone who doesn't believe in Christ, but it isn't that black and white. We first have to look at what it means to be a believer. You could both say you believe in God, but that doesn't mean that you are equally yoked. You can have one person who believes in God but doesn't have a relationship with God, while the other person does have a relationship with God. You can have one person who has a relationship with God and is at church every Sunday, while the other doesn't have a relationship with God, yet is also at church every Sunday. The scenarios are endless. Start by asking if you consider yourself a believer. If so, what does that mean to you?

I (Heather) can tell you that when I first got saved at age twenty, I would have said I was a believer. I did believe in God and that Jesus died for my sins, however, I didn't walk out my relationship with God. I continued to live my life the exact same way, doing and believing the exact same things I had always believed. The only thing that was different for me was that I now had salvation. I lived like that for almost ten years.

It wasn't until I turned thirty that I dedicated my life to God and started on my Christian walk with Him. It was then that I started to know God and started to change my life and live the way He wanted me to live. That included changing foundational beliefs I'd had my entire life—that premarital sex was okay, that the woman always ran the house and finances, and that you should live with someone before you marry them.

If you're walking with God and your date isn't, you aren't going in the same direction. You may think you can start bringing them to church and teaching them about God. That's great and that's what you should do as a Christian, but they may not want to walk in that direction and you can't force them to. You need to recognize that and put on the brakes if you aren't walking together.

Should you ask someone about their beliefs on a first date? I can't give you a yes or no answer on that one. It all depends on whether or not you know the person, where you met, or how the conversation flows. If there is an opportunity to ask, then ask. The last thing you want to do is get into a huge debate over beliefs and religion when there is absolutely no reason to. You can usually get an idea of where someone is at through casual conversation, but sometimes you will have to ask the tough questions.

The Pre-Date Appearance List for Guys

Guys, if you want to attract a woman, you need to know how you are presenting yourself. Your outward appearance has a lot to do with the type of women you attract, as well as how people perceive you. A guy that is well-dressed and well-groomed will be perceived differently than a guy who walks in with his pants on the ground.

I am by no means judging any guy by what he wears. Nor am I insinuating that the clothes make the man. The harsh reality of the world we live in is that people will often judge you by your outward appearance. You don't have to go out and charge up your credit card on a new wardrobe, or be someone you're not. I'm simply saying that there is some truth to the words of the rock band ZZ Top: "Every girl's crazy about a sharp-dressed man."

So, guys, if you're trying to attract a woman who is smart, intelligent, independent, and confident, you better at least look the part yourself. Here is a quick checklist while you are on the lookout for that special someone.

1. Clean your teeth. (If you're missing some, at least brush the ones you have.)

2. Have fresh breath. (Carry mints or gum with you at all times. One sniff of foul breath will end any potential of what could have been.)

3. Use deodorant. (It only takes one stinking time to leave a lasting impression.)

4. Comb your hair. (Don't approach a girl looking like you just rolled out of bed.)

5. Keep your shoulders back and your head up with confidence. (Even if you are shy, you need to practice this. Be confident no matter what.)

6. Don't show up looking like you just rolled out of bed. (Put some thought into what you wear. Pay attention to the details because she will.)

Tips for Navigating Belief Systems

1. What if you are already with someone who isn't a believer?

There are only two choices here: You can leave or stay. If you stay, you know you aren't walking in the same direction and until you start walking together (i.e., their heart changes), either the two of you will get further apart or you will compromise or settle.

2. Look out for the wolf in sheep's clothes!

"Beware of false prophets who come disguised as harmless sheep but are really vicious wolves." (Matthew 7:15 NLT)

Some people know all the Christian lingo and appear to be walking side by side with God, but when you get close to them you see they are far from operating in Christ's love. A wolf is a fox that has learned to be charming. If something doesn't feel right about a person, then it's not right. Call it a feeling in your spirit or your gut; either way, follow it and stay away!

3. What if you are both believers, but your other belief systems aren't the same?

First, determine which of your other beliefs are deal-breakers for you. Then, ask yourself if you are willing to compromise on those deal-breakers, or if you are willing to let God change your heart.

Sharing the Same Values

At the time that Heather and I started dating, we were both Christians but we knew nothing about each other's personal belief systems. Since she vowed not to have sex outside of the marriage covenant again, she wanted to make sure that my beliefs about premarital sex aligned with hers. On the other hand, I was a tither and wanted to make sure that she also believed in supporting the church through financial giving. We both just wanted to make sure that we were walking in agreement with each other.

> "Can two people walk together
> without agreeing on the direction?" Amos 3:3 (NLT)

There were many more things we discussed with each other but the sex and money were the biggest topics, and we're not the only ones who feel that way. It's a known fact that sex and money are two major issues that lead to divorce in today's society.

It's important for you to establish your belief systems and how you can communicate them to the person you are dating. You definitely want to make sure that you don't cause yourself any future problems by not talking about your beliefs in advance.

When we teach the "Dating God's Way" class, we challenge the class to investigate their belief systems by asking questions: What does being a believer mean to you? Does it mean the person goes to church all the time or just every once in a while, or does it mean the person says they have a relationship with God and they don't have to go to church to be a believer? Maybe they grew up in a Christian home and were taught the Bible when they were young, but now they live however they want. Would you be okay with that?

Practical Beliefs

We've talked a lot about belief systems, but it's also important that you discuss your practical beliefs. Believe it or not, it is possible for two Christian people to still have very opposite practical beliefs, which could be destructive in the relationship, if not confronted and dealt with.

What Kind of Dater Are You?

The Casual Dater: This person wants to date different people here and there but doesn't want any strings attached. They are not looking for any type of commitment or future with anyone at this point.

The Serial Dater: This person dates one person after another, whether it's in a committed relationship or a casual one. This person does not like to be alone.

The Rebound Dater: This person has just gone through a breakup and is still hurt from the experience. They never take the time to process their emotions nor heal from a broken heart. In fact, they are still angry with the other person and the only revenge they can take is to start dating someone else so that they can have something to brag about. They might make comments like, "So-and-so walked out of my life so the right person could come along." Now the right person they claim to be dating now has to deal with a hurt, wounded, angry person who is still mad at the last person who just broke up with them.

The Over-Spiritual Dater: This person claims that God told them you are their future spouse after your first date. They not only tell you but they spread the good news to others as well.

The Non-Dater: This person doesn't put themselves out there because they don't want to risk getting hurt or rejected. They keep a guard up at all times so that they won't make the mistake of getting involved with anyone because it might not work out. This person expects for Mr. or Mrs. Right to suddenly appear out of nowhere and sweep them off their feet.

The Stealth Dater: This person dates people on the down low. They don't let other people know they are dating because they have already predetermined the relationship probably won't work out.

I can't express this enough: You need to investigate the other person's beliefs. Let's face it, chances are you and the person you are dating or thinking about dating have come from different backgrounds. They may have been raised differently than you and a lot of their beliefs were instilled into them from their childhood and upbringing. What's normal to you may not be normal to them, and vice versa. You won't know until you take the time to get to know them.

In our dating process, Heather and I spent hours just talking about our belief systems and our life experiences. We were very intentional with our questions. We decided that every time we went out on a date or were just hanging out we would spend a big portion of that time examining our belief systems with each other. We would even write out questions to ask in advance so we would be ready the next time we saw each other.

Discussing Different Backgrounds

We all come from different backgrounds and upbringings, even different church backgrounds. It is through those that we establish most of our belief systems. I (Heather) came from a Catholic background and some of the things I once believed, I no longer believe. My belief system has definitely changed over time, but it is up to you to determine which are set in stone for you and which are not.

We've talked about premarital sex, tithing, respecting leadership, and faith, but what about all those other important topics? What is your belief when it comes to helping others? Raising a family? Your family involvement and the involvement of your family? (These are two completely different things!) Do you believe your children should be homeschooled? Do you believe that you should go to church every Sunday? Do you believe it's important to serve in the church? And why are these so important?

Let's take a look at something as simple as family involvement. What if you aren't close with your family, but the person you are dating is very close with and involved with their family. What if their family is involved with their decision-making or everyday life? That is a belief system that they've grown up with and it may not change. In fact, it may cause a lot of friction and heartache, but at least you know what you are dealing with.

Here are some of the questions that we asked each other during our dating journey:

1. What do you believe a healthy marriage should look like?

This is something that is often overlooked while dating when a couple is so in love and still experiencing the excitement and joy of having a special someone in their lives. Many times, they never even talk about the future because they are so busy enjoying the present. When appropriate, it's important to talk about your expectations of the future in advance, so you can make sure that the two of you are at least on the same page.

2. What is your belief on money management?

This can be a big deal. Remember that money is one of the number one reasons why people get divorced. If your date spends more money than he or she makes and is in debt because of overcharging every credit card, you probably want to make note of that. Heather and I took a look at our strengths and weaknesses when it came to money management and made a decision that if we were to get married, then I would manage our finances. It is still that way even after five years of marriage. Of course, she is still very much a part of the process and we discuss money on a regular basis, but this is a huge area of trust and responsibility on both parts.

3. What is your belief on sex *within* the marriage covenant?

This is a big deal but I would suggest making sure you are at a place in your relationship where you are already advancing further in your journey and you both feel like there is potential for marriage before discussing this one. You also might consider talking to your accountability partner, as well, before proceeding with this conversation.

Here's a prime example of this conversation going wrong if not handled correctly. The guy asks the girl, "What are your beliefs on sex within the marriage covenant?" The girl responds by saying, "I believe that a married couple should have sex at least once a day to keep the marriage healthy." That answer will convince nine out of every ten guys that he's found "The One!" The problem with that is he will have emotional blinders from that moment on and won't pay attention to the fact that she may also believe that being in debt and maxing out credit cards is just a way of life. Six months after the honeymoon, sex won't be as enjoyable or frequent because they are now fighting about money issues.

Unmet expectations are detrimental.

4. What is your belief about having children?

The Bible teaches us to be fruitful and multiply, and that children are a blessing from the Lord. However, you need to decide upfront whether or not you both want to be fruitful and how many times you want to multiply. This is a spiritual matter as well as a practical matter. There are some people who love other people's kids but just don't want to have any of their own.

5. Where do you see yourself in five or ten years?

If one person sees themselves traveling the world, while the other sees themselves at home raising a family, then there could be a serious problem. Now, life may change along the way, but at least you should know that you are heading in the same direction.

6. Do you believe in divorce?

You may think that is too forward of a question but in today's society, many people come from divorced homes and have seen divorce throughout their extended families. In some cases, some people have even been taught that if it doesn't work out, you can always get a divorce and try again.

Confessions of a Long-Term-Relationship Dater

HEATHER'S STORY

I was fifteen years old when I dated my first boyfriend. Thus began my relationship cycle. I would date someone for two or three years and then we would break up. A couple months later, I would find someone else and then I would date him for two or three years. The cycle was still going strong when I met my first husband—we were only married for two years.

I could see the pattern happening, but I couldn't figure out why. I was so focused on *what* these men were doing wrong that I never even considered the *why*. But, when I realized how important it was to me to have a husband and a family, I knew I had to figure out the problem.

I started by looking at the relationship modeled before me: My parents' marriage. Although they were married and lived in the same house, my parents had very separate lives. I could see how their marriage probably contributed to why I continued to end relationships after two or three years, but it didn't answer why I kept starting these relationships.

It wasn't until I sat in a Bible study with some women in my neighborhood that it finally clicked. We were reading a book called *So Long Insecurity* by Beth Moore, and started talking about our past relationships. During that discussion, we discovered an interesting correlation between how much our fathers were involved in our lives and how much we dated. The women whose fathers were encouraging and involved in their lives—not just present—had more fulfilling dating relationships. Why did our fathers' involvement and affection have an impact on our lives? (Notice I use the two words "involvement" and "affection" together. A father can be involved in his daughter's life without being affectionate or vice versa. He can attend all of her school events, but not tell her how much he loves her; or he can tell her he loves her, but be gone traveling most of the year.)

Those of us who went from one unfulfilling relationship to another, whether we dated one man for years or fifteen men within a year—had fathers who weren't involved in our lives. Our fathers were either absent through divorce or living in the same house as us but uninvolved in our lives.

When I was growing up, my father never told me he loved me or that I was pretty or smart (though he does now). He didn't build me up or help me to feel secure. The group of women with involved fathers said their fathers told them that they loved them, they were beautiful, and they were going to be great wives someday.

The women with good marriages and/or dating relationships were the women who looked for a special man who would treat them the way their fathers treated them, instead of dating man after man to gain validation, affirmation, worth, or boost their self-esteem.

Remember ladies, we were created for man; designed to want attention from a man. If we didn't get that attention from our fathers at a young age, we started trying to fill that void when we were old enough to date. That's why it's important for fathers to affirm their daughters, but that's a subject for another book.

The bottom line is this: Whether you are a serial dater, a long-term dater, or have an unfulfilling dating life, it's not too late to change. You are beautiful, smart, valuable, and wonderfully made. If your earthly father did not provide you with what you need, you have a Heavenly Father who will.

> "I praise you because I am fearfully and
> wonderfully made; your works are wonderful.
> I know that full well." (Psalm 139:14 NIV)

PUTTING YOURSELF
OUT THERE

As women, we often think that men are always supposed to chase after us or pursue us. Unfortunately, that no longer is the case. Things have changed. The reality is that men aren't going to just pop into your life. Can it happen? Absolutely, but if you have been waiting for ten or more years, then I hate to break it to you, it may not happen unless *you* make some changes.

Albert Einstein defined insanity as "doing the same thing over and over again and expecting different results." Are you being insane when it comes to dating?

If you want something to happen, you are going to have to do something different. That something can be as simple as sitting in a different row at church or attending a different service. I know that sounds so simple, but we actually had someone from our "Dating God's Way" class who took our advice and made that simple change. She went to a different service, sat in a different row, and actually met her husband. If it worked for her, it can work for you.

If you're looking to meet your mate at church, you have to do more than just attend on a Sunday morning. You are going to have to get involved, meet people, and do things you haven't done before.

Likewise, if you're looking to meet someone while doing something active, look into all of the sports groups, outdoors associations, and gyms in your area. Even if you're shy, you need to be proactive in trying new things so you can be in new situations and surroundings where you can be noticed and where you can talk to people, like these suggestions:

- **Church singles events**
- **Church community groups**
- **Volunteering in your community**
- **Book clubs**
- **Gyms and fitness classes**
- **Athletic leagues**
- **Coffee shops**
- **Dating websites**

You may not meet your mate at these places, but you may meet someone who could be a link to your future relationship. Everyone knows someone who is single! You really have to explore every avenue: Get out there and be an active participant.

I read something once that said, "You have to market yourself. You can't just sit in your house waiting for all the singles to surround your house, waiting for you to come out." It sounds funny, but if you haven't dated anyone in a very long time, that's exactly what you are doing—you just haven't had anyone call you out on it.

So, how do you market yourself? Marketing is really selling yourself, promoting yourself, and getting noticed. First, you need to put your sign up. When you want to sell a home, you put a sign up in the front yard to let everyone know the house is available. When you are single and looking to date, you need to make sure it is clear that you are available.

Now, there is a difference between showing you're single and being desperate. Putting yourself out there and trying new things is not being desperate. Chasing after someone is being desperate. Dating someone who doesn't share your same foundational beliefs is being desperate. Overlooking all the red flags when dating someone is being desperate.

Let's look a little more at putting your sign up and making sure it says what you think it says. Every person gives off an available or unavailable vibe. If you are available and looking, then you need to have your sign up.

Contrary to what you'd think, if you are too confident or too comfortable you may appear unavailable. If you are too confident, it may seem like you don't need or want anyone and that can make you look unavailable. You may not "need" anyone, but if you desire to have someone then you have to at least look available.

We've all heard someone say, "They let themselves go after they got married." If you look like you've let yourself go, then maybe you are a little too comfortable. Find people who you know will tell you the truth, and ask them about whether or not your sign is up.

For Ladies Only

Here are some practical things to consider when heading out on the town:

- Put a smile on your face!
- Look in the mirror before you go out and make sure you're holding up the kind of sign that will attract who you want to attract. (Ladies, if you are wearing a low-cut shirt, you may be attracting someone who is hoping to see more.)
- Make eye contact when talking to someone.
- Hold your head up high and walk with confidence.
- If you are in a slump, reinvent yourself and your look.
- Be optimistic. Negativity is never attractive.
- Love yourself!

I know some of these are so simple, but sometimes we forget to do them. The fact is, you just never know when or where you will meet someone.

Let's also look at what kind of sign you are holding up. If you are in your mid-thirties, does your sign say mid-thirties, or is it more like that of someone in their mid-forties or mid-twenties? Do your clothing, hair, makeup, and attitude give you the appearance of being older or younger? If so, are you okay with attracting someone older or younger? If you look like you don't care about your appearance, are you okay with dating someone who doesn't look like they care about their appearance? It all depends on what you are comfortable with and who you are attracted to.

Here's something I've heard many times: If you are looking for someone with a six-pack, then you need to have a six-pack. If you are looking for someone to do Bible studies with, then you need to be doing Bible studies. In other words, you shouldn't expect more from someone than you expect from yourself. Your best chance of finding someone is to make sure who you are attracting lines up with who you are attracted to.

I've heard from women especially, "A man needs to like me for who I am." That is true because over time looks do fade. But, first, you have to attract him so he'll want to get to know you more. In other words, you have to put out bait for him to bite the hook. And that goes for both men and women.

I had a friend who always went to the grocery store in her sweats, without combing her hair or putting on makeup. She was single and I warned her that was probably not the best idea, considering she had her eyes on a man who worked down the street.

Lo and behold, the man walked up to her one day in the frozen food section and started talking to her. She was mortified! She couldn't even look him in the eye or have a normal conversation. She had her chance and she blew it.

Appearance is more than what you look like. It's also how you carry yourself. If you aren't carrying yourself with confidence, ask yourself why. If you need a makeover, ask a friend whose sense of style you trust to help you out. If you need a pep talk, sit down and write a list of all of your great qualities, hang it on your mirror, and remind yourself every day until you are confident in yourself.

Everything in life requires you to be an active participant, yet when it comes to dating we seem to forget that. Everything God asks of you requires you to be an active participant too. You don't just sit there and receive. You have to go out there and fight for what you want.

If you have the desire to be married, you have to go out there in search of your future spouse. Don't just sit at home Monday through Saturday, go to church on Sunday, and expect to find "The One." I can't stress this enough—you aren't going to find someone without being an active participant. If you keep doing what you've always done, you're going to keep getting what you've always gotten; and if nothing is all you've ever gotten, nothing is exactly what you're going to keep getting.

To Pursue or Be Pursued

So, you've found someone you're interested in, now how do you get them to notice you?

Show that interest! Letting someone know you are available by showing interest is not the same as pursuing them; you're merely making your presence known in their world.

If they are in a certain life group, get involved in that life group. If they have a group of good friends, get into that circle of friends. It's okay to find out more about someone who's caught your eye. Go hang out in a group and start a conversation with that person. Let him know that you are available. Let her know that you may be interested.

If he likes baseball, set up a group event to a baseball game and invite him. What is it going to hurt? If he says no, then you go to the baseball game and have a good time. If he says yes, then it's the perfect opportunity to get to know him a little better.

If she likes Saturday morning coffee at her local coffee shop, show up there and say hello. After all, she isn't a stranger at this point; this is someone you know a little about already. She may even invite you to sit down.

Pursuing: The Good and the Bad

Taking an active role, such as becoming involved in a group or activity in order to get to know someone better, is not pursuing;

it's being proactive. Pursuing is when you take the initiative to ask someone out on a date and go out together, and then you continue asking and initiating.

You can also pursue the wrong way, like when a woman keeps calling or texting and not giving the man a chance to pursue her, even though he is interested. Another example would be when a man isn't interested in a woman, yet she keeps inviting him out or calling or texting. Or when a man continues to pursue her after a woman has made it clear she's not interested.

What if there are mixed signals? Sometimes men and women continue to pursue because they honestly think there's interest or potential there, when the other party is really being nice and doesn't want to hurt anyone's feelings. In the end, this behavior doesn't help anyone and only hurts the situation.

If someone is pursuing you and you have no interest, let them know. If you are showing a little interest because you're still deciding if you like the person, that's great. If you are showing a lot of interest because you simply don't want to hurt the other person's feelings, that's not good!

Go back to mine and Adonis's dating story: When Adonis asked me to join his life group, he'd already done his research and knew I liked golf. It was also a safe environment for him to talk to me. He wouldn't need to feel personally rejected if I didn't want to go golfing. After all, I wouldn't be rejecting him, just the plans to go golfing.

It wasn't until after I showed up, golfed, and had conversation with him that he decided he wanted to get to know me better and invited me to come out the driving range again. From that point on, he pursued me, but that didn't mean I sat around and made him do all the work; I had to be an active participant. I had to let him know that I was interested and wanted to get to know him more too.

Just like women have different personalities, so do men. Some men are shy and need to know that you are interested before they ask you out.

Ladies, if you have someone you are interested in, invite him out to a group event. Send him a message and let him know that a group of people are going out to a movie or a concert and that he is welcome to come. That doesn't mean he has to go and it doesn't mean that you are pursuing him. You've simply opened the door and, at that point, if he starts pursuing you, great! If he doesn't, then he's probably not interested and you don't need to chase him down.

6 Things to Avoid Doing on a First Date

1. Going to a fancy restaurant. (If you aren't comfortable at a fancy restaurant, then you can't be yourself.)

2. Going to a loud concert. (You can't even hear yourself, so how can you hear someone else?)

3. Going to a movie. (It's kind of impossible get to know someone during a movie.)

4. Introducing them to any members of your family. (That's just plain awkward for anyone on a first date.)

5. Anything illegal. (It's a very bad impression to end a first date in jail.)

6. Spending a lot of money trying to impress your date. (This will set up an expectation that you may not be able to uphold.)

WHAT DO YOU EXPECT?

The Importance of Stating Your Expectations

Expectations are commonly overlooked by dating couples or engaged couples about to be married. The couple is so in love that they forget to express their expectations of one another in a marital relationship. I can't tell you how many times I've been in a counseling session with a married couple going through difficulties in their relationship all because of unmet expectations.

Spouses often say, "This is not what I signed up for," or "I never expected it to be like this." That's partly true because they never took the time to express their expectations before they said the words "I do."

The other part is because their spouse never knew what they expected and therefore has no idea that they are not living up to the expectations. Now, one of them is upset because their experience in the marriage isn't what they expected.

We've all encountered events that just don't quite meet our expectations. For example, let's say there's a restaurant you've heard so many great things about. You look it up online and are elated as you read the reviews and look at the pictures of the food. You make reservations and can't wait to go. When you finally show up, the parking is horrible. The place is uncomfortably crowded. The temperature inside the restaurant is so cold that you wish you had worn your parka. To make things worse, you have to wait an extra thirty minutes just to be seated because the restaurant is running behind schedule with their reservations. Before you even sit down, you're an unhappy customer who feels as if you just got the raw end of the deal, so when your food finally comes out, you can't even enjoy what would have probably been the best meal you've ever eaten. Long story short, you leave the restaurant saying, "Well, this is not what I expected!"

This is just a hypothetical scenario, but let's look at it with a different perspective. What if when you called to make the reservations you stated your expectations in addition to that? What if you told them that you wanted valet parking when you showed up at 7:30 p.m.? You also instructed them to make sure the room temperature was at a comfortable 72 degrees. And finally, you wanted to be seated right away because you don't ever like to wait, especially when you've taken the time to make reservations. They may have told you to try the restaurant down the street, but you can see my point. At least you would have stated your expectations and given the place a chance to meet them, instead of keeping them to yourself.

Dating can be just like that. You can't be afraid to let the other person know what you expect of them as you continue on this journey. It's not being controlling; it's giving them a clear picture of what the future looks like in your mind. It provides the option to either rise up and meet those expectations, or point you to the restaurant down the street.

A Few Tips on Stating Your Expectations

1. Be clear and concise. Leave no room for interpretation. If you are not clear, you are leaving room for an unpleasant experience.

2. Use your expectations as guardrails while you're dating. If you can see the dating experience start to drift outside of your expectations, you must state them again.

3. Keep it real. Make sure your expectations are attainable and will only set the relationship up for success.

You don't need to micro-manage the person you are dating. No one likes that. Either they will meet your expectations or they won't. And not meeting your expectations doesn't mean that they are a bad person. It just means they did not meet your expectations in a certain area.

Write down at least five expectations you have regarding a dating relationship or a future marriage:

1._____

2._____

3._____

4. _____

5. _____

BOUNDARIES FOR PHYSICAL CONTACT:

Yes, They Absolutely Matter

Boundaries and guidelines should matter to you because they keep you and those around you safe everyday. If you drive a vehicle, you stay within the boundaries of those center stripes on the road to keep you from crossing over into oncoming traffic. The moment you go outside those boundaries, you immediately sense that you are in a danger zone and could potentially harm yourself and/or others and instantly self-correct back into your lane so no accidents take place. If only we could feel that same kind of immediate danger when we step outside of God's boundaries for our relationships.

Even though it totally goes against the Word of God; some Christians do engage in premarital sex.

"Now the works of the flesh are evident, which are:
adultery, fornication, uncleanness, lewdness, idolatry,
sorcery, hatred, contentions, jealousies, outbursts
of wrath, selfish ambitions, dissensions, heresies."
(Galatians 5:19–20 NKJV)

Fornication is the voluntary sexual intercourse between two unmarried persons or two persons not married to each other. While the Bible clearly assigns the act of fornication to our sinful nature, better known as our flesh, some Christians still have or will have premarital sex. Yes, it happens. I'm not excusing it; just stating a fact.

Whether Christian or non-Christian, if you're alone with the person you have feelings for and you start getting physical, it has the potential to open up the door for something to happen.

A Story from a Guy's Point of View

I remember attending a young men's small group studying relationships with the opposite sex. One young man raised his hand and asked the question, "What do you do if you're alone with your girlfriend and things start getting hot and heavy and she takes off her clothes?"

I will never forget the group leader's answer. He said, "If you don't run, you're in trouble." Man, how things would have been different for me if I would have taken that advice literally.

Looking back on my pre-Christian years, I didn't really date a lot of girls and I never had sex, even when a girl I was dating wanted to. In fact, one girlfriend broke up with me because I *wouldn't* have sex with her, which seems rare these days. But the moment I became a Christian, it seemed liked all of a sudden girls were attracted to me and I ended up having sex with a girlfriend.

My first sexual encounter didn't happen immediately, but over time. Little by little, we pushed the envelope. It started with us making out for long periods of time at her place. I felt like that was okay since we didn't have sex. We would even pray before and after making out, which, in reality was only an attempt to ease our consciences. Then the physical contact became more and more aggressive with touching. Every time it left me wanting more and more. Eventually, that led to taking off items of clothing, and after that, it was like trying to stop a runaway train.

The sex felt good but that feeling couldn't hold a candle to the overwhelming conviction. It took me weeks to get over the feeling of disappointing God.

Let's face it, men, we are wired to be attracted to women. No matter how strong you think you are, when you find yourself in the wrong place at the wrong time, all of the strength and self-control you think you have can easily fly out the window.

And ladies, please make note of this. A lot of Christian single women say they are looking for a godly man. You may find one and if you do, that's great. Just keep in mind that your godly man is still a man, with manly appetites. I may be the only guy you will ever hear this from, but ladies—men need your help to stay strong. In other words, if you are making out with your "godly man" without giving him any boundaries or off-limit places to your anatomy, then something else just might happen that the both of you will regret.

Now, don't get me wrong. The guy needs to take responsibility, too, but there are certain scenarios that you, as a woman, can help us men avoid. For instance, let's say you're dating a man and you like him to cuddle with you. It's probably not a good thing for you to invite him to cuddle in your bed. Trust me, whether he admits it or not, that will awaken some appetites in him. It's kind of like bringing a lion into a meat market and saying, "Sit, boy. Good lion."

In the Bible, there's the very familiar story of King David and Bathsheba. Chances are you've heard it once or twice, whether you go to church or not. It's found in the book of Second Samuel chapters eleven and twelve.

In the spring of the year, when kings normally go out to war, David sent Joab and the Israelite army to fight the Ammonites. They destroyed the Ammonite army and laid siege to the city of Rabbah. However, David stayed behind in Jerusalem.

Late one afternoon, after his midday rest, David got out of bed and was walking on the roof of the palace. As he looked out over the city, he noticed a woman of unusual beauty taking a bath. He sent someone to find out who she was, and he was told, "She is Bathsheba, the daughter of Eliam and the wife of Uriah the Hittite." Then David sent messengers to get her; and when she came to the palace, he slept with her. (2 Samuel 11:1–4 NLT)

When reading this for the first time, I have two obvious responses:

1. King David never should have been out on his rooftop. He should have been out to war with the rest of the kings.
2. What the heck was Bathsheba doing taking a bath outside? Talk about instant attraction for any guy.

Many Christians and Theologians draw disagreeing opinions and assumptions about this story. Some believe Bathsheba was taking a bath inside her house and David knew the rooftop gave him the advantage of being a peeping tom. Others believe she was bathing naked outside when David innocently just happened to see her and was overcome by lust. You can form your own opinion, but the real truth may never be known because we were not there with David and Bathsheba and, even if we were, we can't know what's in another person's heart. Personally, I think that both people could have simply been in the wrong place at the wrong time.

Your body has the ability to get out of control and you can do something even though in your mind and heart you know it's wrong. After you've done it once, then it's so easy to let it become a repeated cycle. I've been here before and I know a lot of Christian guys have as well.

You sincerely love God but you keep ending up in these compromising situations of fulfilling the desires of your flesh. You feel awful afterwards but before long, you become numb to that feeling. That's an out of control, dangerous place; a place where you stop listening to the right voices of influence and you try desperately to keep your hidden lifestyle a secret. Trust me, that's not a good place to be and the longer you stay there, the worse things will get.

I found freedom from that place through reaching out to other men for help and guidance. If you are going through some of the things I have just described, then I want to encourage you to reach out to someone you trust for help. Sometimes it's easier to find your way out of something when the road has already been paved by others.

We talked earlier about the importance of having an accountability partner. I suggest this accountability partner be a man that you trust and look up to. Maybe you could find someone to confide in or talk to in your church leadership. Chances are that whoever that man is, he will be able to identify with some of your struggles because, as I said earlier, we men are all wired alike. He will be able to help navigate through this area of your life, but it will take more than just listening to him; you'll also need to heed his advice. Be encouraged and know that this battle is not uncommon, nor is it unfamiliar, but it is a battle that can be conquered.

I am also aware that there are women who deal with this; who have sexual encounters with different men one after another, all the while not being able to figure out why they are reliving this pattern again and again. Some may feel that it's a way to keep a guy, especially if they fear losing him. Others may like having sex just as much as guys do and don't see anything wrong with it. Sooner or later, however, they come to a place where they realize how they feel or how others perceive them, and they want to change. If that's you, then you will need a strong accountability partner to help you navigate these new feelings and emotions. I encourage you to reach out to a woman you trust and respect, and begin to open up and share your situation.

It happens over and over: A guy and girl meet, fall in love, and start planning a future together. But what if they don't share the same values and boundaries? Imagine that the young lady has been saving herself for marriage and she meets a wonderful guy—the guy she thinks is "The One." If he doesn't share her view that sex should be reserved for marriage, there are quite a few possible scenarios that can play out, not all of which are favorable.

Scenario 1: She stands her ground and doesn't have premarital sex.

Response 1: He accepts and respects her view and they work together to make sure this is honored.

Response 2: He doesn't agree with her view, may pressure her to change her mind, and the relationship ends.

Scenario 2: She finally concedes and has premarital sex, thinking that since they'll be married anyway, what's the big deal?

Response 1: This may cause guilt that could have been avoided, but they can still work through this and practice sexual purity until marriage.

Response 2: If both parties aren't fully invested in this relationship, there might be feelings of remorse, the feeling of being trapped, or one person can end the relationship.

Yes, relationships can be very emotional, especially when you're talking about the future, commitments, and love. But boundaries are there for a reason. They're also meant to stand without exception. Your emotions cannot dictate when it's okay to step outside of a boundary. Once you overstep a boundary, there's usually danger waiting for you on the other side.

A couple could have strong feelings for each other and feel like they are going to get married. But wrong thinking doesn't produce right actions. Acting like you're married *before* you're married can lead to trouble.

In the Beginning...There Were Boundaries

It's so important in a dating relationship to stick with the boundaries you set in the beginning. They are there to keep you away from potentially compromising situations.

When Heather and I were dating, she lived with a family from our church. Both Ted and Charity loved us very much and wanted to make sure that we didn't make mistakes along the way, so they set boundaries for us. I wasn't allowed upstairs in her room and they set a curfew for us when we went out.

My initial reaction was, "You gotta be kidding me!" This was very hard at first. Ted and I were friends and golfing buddies long before Heather and I started dating and now he was telling me what to do.

One time we were out on a date and were running late to meet our 10:30 p.m. curfew. We were like two panicking teenagers! I told her to call Ted and Charity to tell them we would be a little late. We were only ten minutes late when we finally pulled up in front of the house, but Ted was standing out in the driveway like an angry father ready to bring correction. He walked up to the vehicle, opened Heather's door, helped her out of the car, closed the door, and walked her inside. He didn't even acknowledge me!

I can laugh about it now but as we both look back, we see the importance of those boundaries and how they played a huge role in the success of our marriage today. Needless to say, I never brought her home late again and yes, Ted and I are still friends.

Boundaries are your friend. If you're going to date God's way then you, too, will need some boundaries.

There are different types of boundaries and each couple's boundaries are unique to their relationship. However, it is very important to have certain fundamental boundaries set that keep your flesh out of compromising situations.

> "Keep watch and pray, so that you will not
> give in to temptation. For the spirit is willing,
> but the body is weak." (Mark 14:38 NLT)

Boundaries help us keep watch because our body is weak and when we put ourselves into compromising situations, it can be difficult to not give in. Please don't deceive yourself in this area. I heard a wise man say it like this, "It's easier to stop a speeding locomotive than it is to stop two half-naked bodies from going all the way."

Remember, it's important to have boundaries established *before* you get too head-over-heels in love with someone. Set these boundaries now while your mind and heart are not influenced by the thought of holding onto that special someone. If you're already in a relationship, an honest evaluation of how things are going can help you establish some boundaries or set new boundaries if needed.

Take some time to write down these boundaries and think of them as the extension of the Ten Commandments:

_____

_____

_____

_____

_____

_____

_____

PITFALLS OF
LIVING TOGETHER

Many people view living together as a way to safeguard and protect themselves against a possible mistake of marrying the wrong person. In actuality, it only reduces your ability to have and enjoy healthy dating relationships.

In today's society, the media is oversaturated with what I (Adonis) call an anti-God relationship view. Think about it. When was the last time you saw a married couple in a love scene on television? Many of today's television shows are all about couples living together and having premarital sex—don't forget the big hook-up mentality. The media rarely shows the aftermath of damaged emotions, broken hearts, and dysfunctional relationships that are all byproducts of sexual immorality and hooking up.

But What if It's Easier on Finances?

Maybe you're on the fence about not having premarital sex. Society, and probably most people you ask (even some Christians), will say that living together before marriage is okay. Most people even suggest it.

There is *no scripture* that says that you can't live with someone you're dating. However, when you live with someone, you take away all of your guardrails. You are fooling yourself if you think you can live together and spend every night in close proximity with someone you are emotionally invested in and physically attracted to, and not have things change between you. That change may be a physical line you cross or an emotional line you cross that you weren't meant to cross.

One of the reasons unmarried couples move in together is because of their financial situation. To that I (Heather) say: You need to have faith that God will provide for and take care of you. You may also need to make some changes in your finances. You don't want to make a temporary choice that can affect a lifetime. Dating a year or two is temporary compared to a lifetime marriage.

You want to set yourself up for a good marriage. If that means one or both of you have to have a different roommate, then do it! Take away the temptation and put up the guardrails so you don't fail. If you honor God, He will bless you. You'll have plenty of time to live with someone when you're married.

I lived with my ex-husband before we got married because everyone said we had to make sure we were compatible and that we could get along 24/7. We got married and nothing changed. Part of me was expecting it to be different somehow, but it wasn't. It was just like any other past relationship I'd had and we had problems that we couldn't resolve, even though we had a "trial run" before we got married.

Adonis and I didn't live together before we got married and

it was completely different. It was a new journey. It was fun and exciting. We got along just fine 24/7 and still do!

Most Common Reasons Why Couples Live Together

1. We're engaged and going to get married anyway.

Our Opinion: Why not wait and keep the door shut to the enemy? Enjoy sex within the holy covenant of God.

2. We don't want to sign another six-month lease when we're going to be married in a few short months. It's cheaper for us to live together instead of paying for two places, and allows us to save money.

Our Opinion: That's a big risk. A six-month lease is cheaper than divorce court. Research indicates that people who live together prior to getting married are more likely to have marriages that end in divorce.

3. We want to give this a test-drive first.

Our Opinion: You test-drive cars, not people. No one develops a soul tie with an automobile, unless you're the guy from the movie *Christine*. It's easier to walk away from a car deal than it is to walk away from someone you have a soul tie with.

Although the Bible doesn't state that dating couples should not live together, it does caution us against sexual immorality.

> "Flee sexual immorality. Every sin that a man does is
> outside the body, but he who commits sexual immorality
> sins against his own body." (1 Corinthians 6:18 NKJV)

> "Shun immorality *and* all sexual looseness [flee from
> impurity in thought, word, or deed]. Any other sin

which a man commits is one outside the body, but he
who commits sexual immorality sins against his own
body." (1 Corinthians 6:18 AMP, emphasis mine)

Sometimes I think that "Thou shalt not live together before marriage" should have been the Eleventh Commandment. Living together is a perfect set-up for sexual immorality—a set-up for a total mess-up. Don't fool yourself. It's hard to flee sexual activity or thoughts when you're constantly living under the same roof and being tempted on a daily basis.

When I (Adonis) have been in coaching sessions with dating Christian couples that have chosen to live together first, they usually give me at least one of the reasons listed above. However, they quickly respond by saying, "We are not sleeping together or having sex." As a pastor, I can respond one of two ways. I can respond as a pastor by saying, "Well, praise the Lord! Glad to know that both of you are stronger than Superman." Or I can respond as a peer by saying, "Yeah right. How's that working for you?" Regardless of my response, the couple has chosen to place themselves in a very compromising situation that often leads to sexual immorality.

Heather brings another perspective and challenging thought to couples that are living together but say they are not having sex. Her perspective is, if you are a dating couple, living together, and not having sex, then maybe you're not physically attracted to one another and that will no doubt be a pitfall for any potential marriage. It definitely gives you something to think about.

Once again, we are not condoning sexual immorality and we are not saying that it is impossible to live together without having sex. We are just keeping it real by stating a fact that few people are strong enough to abstain when the opportunity presents itself everyday, especially if you are sleeping in the same bed or showering in the same living space.

By living together before marriage, you open yourself up to sexual sin, which produces strong soul-ties (which bind two people together spiritually) and emotional ties that also bind you to that person. If the relationship doesn't work out, then you're on a long journey to break free from the soul-ties that were created while you two were "living together."

SEXUAL PURITY:

What Does It Mean?
How Does It Work?

Sex was created by God and can be enjoyed without the guilt, shame, or consequences when it's done within the marriage covenant. When the act of sex takes place outside of the marriage covenant, it opens up the door for a snowball effect of emotions, problems, and feelings of guilt and shame. It also creates soul ties, which we mentioned earlier.

God created sex with the intent of bringing a husband and wife into union with one another. The act of sex, whether within or outside of the marriage covenant, still produces what God intended for it to produce and brings two people into spiritual union with one another.

God is a forgiving God and, yes, there is forgiveness of sexual sin. The big problem is that sometimes it takes weeks, months, or even years to get free from the soul ties and baggage that came along with it. That's why God forewarns us in His Word to run from sexual sin. You must learn to recognize any potential set-ups or circumstances that could give an opportunity for this line to be crossed. There are some things that you just absolutely should not do when you're in a dating relationship and trying to keep it sexually pure.

Years ago, I counseled a young couple that crossed a line that they never thought they would. They never intended on having sex outside of marriage but they did and now they were both dealing with the fallout of their actions. They didn't feel like Christians anymore. Each one blamed the other for not being strong enough to stop. They went from two people who loved each other to two people who were embarrassed to look at each other. They felt like they had disappointed God and He would never forgive them. The real truth was that they struggled to forgive themselves.

In the midst of the counseling session, I asked them what things led up to the act of sexual activity. They both agreed that it was being physical little by little, and increased from there: Spending late nights at each other's place. Make-out sessions that lasted way too long. Each time they went a little further until they lost sight of the boundaries because it felt so good. The last comment in that session is the one I want to drive home. She said, "Everything felt so good until the moment was over, then everything came crashing down. There was guilt, shame, ugliness, and a feeling of total disappointment." And he agreed.

That's the trick of the enemy; how many lives and relationships are ruined because of this? I am convinced that if there were a way to feel the end results before the act, then a lot of people would avoid premarital sex.

Please don't take this the wrong way, but prayer alone is not the only thing to help you stay free from sexual sin. You can pray all day long, "God, keep me pure," but if you are constantly putting yourself in heated moments of passion with the person you are dating, then your flesh will eventually take over. Your prayer needs to be, "God, please show me the things to avoid doing that have the potential to trip me up in this area."

Keep Safeguards in Place

I believe there are some practical things that can safeguard and ensure our pursuit of sexual purity. Here are a few examples:

1. Keep your clothes on no matter what.

Trust me, nothing good can happen with your clothes off unless you are married. If you want to keep it clean, keep your clothes on. My Sunday school teacher used to say, No skin, no sin. Seriously, this is an area that we often underestimate. Once you cross that line, it's like firing up the jet engines on a 747.

2. Avoid long make-out sessions.

Long make-out sessions can turn into sexual obsession. Know your limit and then stay about a mile away from it. Seriously, Christian or non-Christian, your flesh, when out of control, can become unstoppable. Have a list of prerequisites if you are going to kiss or make-out. Kissing standing up in a well-lit area is a lot different from kissing on your bed or sofa in the dark. It's so easy for a situation to get out of hand in a matter of seconds.

3. No sleepovers.

Sleepovers are for children. You are an adult and your hormones are further advanced. Don't try to prove to each other or anyone else that you are strong and can abstain from sex. That's insane! It would be easier for a five-year-old to turn down a big piece of birthday cake than for you to keep your hands to yourself while in bed together at night wearing the bare minimum. This also causes others, once they find out, to see your relationship in a negative way. The Bible talks about avoiding the appearance of evil.

4. Communicate with your accountability partner.

We discussed the importance of accountability early on. That person is there to help guide you in your relationship. When you are feeling strong urges or desires they can help reinforce the boundaries and offer wisdom and sound coaching. When you can't see the obvious because you are too emotionally involved, they are able to bring sound counsel in the midst of your feelings.

5. If all else fails…

Put the big Family Bible (the one with the picture of Jesus on it) between the two of you.

Society's View of Sexual Purity

I (Heather) was raised in a Catholic home and learned that sex was okay as long you were in love. It didn't have to be in the covenant of marriage. It was okay to live together before marriage—even encouraged—because you can't truly know someone until you live with them. I was never taught that sexual purity was something you should do or that it was even possible.

In society today, there is nothing that says you should live a sexually pure life. When was the last time you saw a husband and wife having sex on a TV show or movie? It's always couples that aren't married. Society definitely pushes that image and it's been like that for a long time.

Even as Christians, we've somehow lost or skipped over that part of the Bible. We believe other things in the Bible, but we say God didn't intend sexual purity for us, or that was written back in the old days.

Because of my background and society, I had a hard time understanding the truth. When I got saved it was a process; one of the things God showed me was the importance of living a sexually pure life.

Still struggling to understand why, I really prayed about this. One day I was having a conversation with a friend who is a Christian and I asked her thoughts on the topic. She explained it like this: "You know, Heather, I have children and I love them so much. They want to play in the street because it's more fun than playing in the yard. As a parent, I don't want to take away their fun. I also don't want them playing out in the street because I don't want them getting hurt. It's for their protection."

At that moment, I understood because I remember wanting to play in the street as a kid. I thought my parents were just being mean, but now, being a parent myself, I completely understand. It's common sense. Still, for some reason we have a hard time accepting God's protection in this area of our lives.

God loves us very much and doesn't want us to get hurt. That is why He has said sex is for the covenant of marriage, where it is protected and safe.

"Run from sexual sin! No other sin so clearly affects
the body as this one does. For sexual immorality is a
sin against your own body." (1 Corinthians 6:18 NLT)

God put this in the Bible for a reason. If you enter into a sexual relationship that is not in the covenant of marriage, someone is going to get hurt. You may not be the person getting hurt, but you may be hurting someone.

God created sex as a form of unity, the only time that a man and a woman can physically be one with each other. The soul tie connects you. When you become one with one another outside the covenant of marriage and then try to break that soul tie, you will feel the emotional burden of it—a loss.

You also don't realize the emotional damage that can cause. Especially as women, we are very emotional beings. To have a connection like that and then have that connection broken will lead to feelings of abandonment or rejection and feeling paralyzed in moving forward. God wants to protect us from unnecessarily feeling those hurts and emotions.

There's more to sex than mere skin on skin. Sex is as much spiritual mystery as physical fact. As written in scripture, "The two become one." Since we want to become spiritually one with the Master, we must not pursue the kind of sex that avoids commitment and intimacy, leaving us more lonely than ever—the kind of sex that can never "become one." There is a sense in which sexual sins are different from all others. In sexual sin we violate the sacredness of our own bodies, these bodies that were made for God-given and God-modeled love, for "becoming one" with another. Or didn't you realize that your body is a sacred place, the place of the Holy Spirit? Don't you see that you can't live however you please, squandering what God paid such a high price for? The physical part of you is not some piece of property belonging to the spiritual part of you. God owns the whole works. So let people see God in and through your body. (1 Corinthians 6:16–20 MSG)

But Everyone Else Is Doing It

Nowadays people who aren't having premarital sex are in the minority. But if you look at the marriages of people who didn't have premarital sex and the ones that did, I bet the people that didn't have premarital sex have a better sex life. I would go so far as to say a better marriage, too, because so much respect and trust was shown. Those are the things that you need to consider and look at when you decide which route you want to take in your relationship.

I've counseled with women who are about to get married and they ask me how marriage is different. "What's left for the marriage?" You can be in a sexual relationship with someone and then you get married and nothing changes. You may be looking for a wow factor and it doesn't come. That can start your marriage off with disappointment.

If you remain sexually pure up until your wedding night, then you can experience the wow factor. Plus, you want God to bless you in this area of your marriage. The top reasons for divorce are due to sex, money, and children. Why not eliminate the sex one right from the get-go?

I've often heard that the devil tries to get you into bed before you're married and tries to get you out of bed once you are married. That is true, but why? The devil wants to drive a wedge between you and God because he knows we feel disappointment when we let God down. Also, he wants us to feel insecure. If we know that a person can leave us, it leads to feelings of insecurity and mistrust. If he or she is willing to cross the line or give into their flesh with you, then he or she may be willing to give into their flesh with someone else. If they were weak with you then they may be weak if put into a compromising situation.

If you express to someone that sexual purity is important to you and that you want to keep your relationship right with God, then you want someone who will admire and respect that. If you falter or they push you, then that is going to cause some trust issues. If they respect you and your relationship with God, then they won't want to see that relationship with God harmed.

If they don't respect you or your relationship with God enough to wait, then what other beliefs are they not going to respect? You want someone who you can trust to follow through with their beliefs. If they show you they can be trustworthy outside of the marriage covenant, then most likely they will be trustworthy inside of the marriage covenant.

What if I'm Not a Virgin?

Some of you may be thinking, "I've already ruined that because I'm no longer a virgin." Sexual purity doesn't mean that you are a virgin. It means that, no matter what your past is, you are now committed to remaining sexually pure until marriage. God has already forgiven us for our past mistakes.

> "This means that anyone who belongs to Christ has
> become a new person. The old life is gone; a new life
> has begun!" (2 Corinthians 5:17 NLT)

You may already be practicing sexual purity or this may be completely new to you. Either way, you are going to have to set up guardrails or boundaries.

Adonis and I didn't discuss these on the first, second, or third date, but waited until we were comfortable enough with each other to discuss this issue. We started with an obvious one: We were not allowed to spend the night together. If this hits a nerve with you, and you've done this in the past, ask yourself what path that lead you down. Exactly! We know what path it led us down and that's why we implemented it.

Not only were we not allowed to spend the night together, he wasn't even allowed in my bedroom. Not even in the middle of the day when someone else was home. I know these seem strict, but we wanted to ensure that we didn't cross the line. Think about it, you have two people who care for each other on an emotional level and are attracted to each other on a physical level. If you add isolation and a bed, what do you get? A recipe for disaster!

This is especially true if you have already awakened your sexual side. My pastor, Jillian Chambers, has described it as waking a baby. Once you awaken it, you need to care for it, nurture it, and feed it. That part of us isn't meant to be awakened until we are in the protected covenant of marriage. Just like a baby, once you have awakened it, you have to work to put it back to sleep. This usually happens by changing your belief system. The other part of the battle is to keep it asleep. That's where you have to set these strict rules or boundaries.

As you recall, Ted and Charity, my roommates, wanted to help us too. They gave me a curfew and enforced it! The fact is that the later in the night, the more tired you become. When you are tired, you start to make bad decisions or at least let your guard down. Plus, it's easier to hide things in the dark. The reality is that there is nothing we can hide from God.

Moving on from Casual Sex with Multiple Partners

Having multiple partners outside of the marriage covenant leaves you wounded, lost, confused, and hurting. It also can leave you so calloused that sex with anyone becomes just a normal activity.

So, over time and with multiple partners, a person is left feeling numb and void of true feelings. This person, in turn, is no longer able to recognize or even respond to true love when it comes along.

> "Don't you realize that your bodies are actually
> parts of Christ? Should a man take his body, which is
> part of Christ, and join it to a prostitute? Never!
> And don't you realize that if a man joins himself to
> a prostitute, he becomes one body with her? For the
> scriptures say, 'The two are united into one.'"
> (1 Corinthians 6:15–16 NLT)

If you've found yourself in this position and you don't know what to do, then a good place to start your healing process is to invite God into the situation.

Dealing with the Aftermath of Divorce

In a covenant relationship, when a married couple comes together intimately, their souls touch and mingle together, becoming one. This was God's plan and intention from the very beginning and still is—bringing two people together and joining them as one.

"This explains why a man leaves his father and mother
and is joined to his wife, and the two are united
into one" (Matthew 19:5 NLT)

This is why divorce is so painful. When two married people have been joined together and then go through a divorce, there is a physical, emotional, and spiritual separation.

Divorce leaves open wounds, damaged emotions, painful memories, and calloused scars. However, there is life after divorce. Through time, God can provide healing, recovery, and restoration to your soul.

I Messed Up. Now What? Getting Back on Track with Sexual Purity

There is no perfect relationship out there. Each one is different and they each have their own ups and downs. Even when both people are Christians and trying to avoid temptations, if safeguards and boundaries are not in place in the area of sexual purity, there is always that chance of crossing the line. This may be contrary to popular belief, but a one-time act of premarital sex does not doom the relationship to failure if it's a one-time mistake. (No, that doesn't give you a free pass!) However, it does make things a lot harder and more complicated if the couple continues in this manner.

If you desire to date in accordance to sexual purity, you will need to strive to stay on target in this area. But, if you cross the line in a weak moment, there is still hope. If you both are sincere and truly sorry for your actions, then there are a couple of things you need to do in order to get your relationship back on track and headed in the right direction.

Porn Has No Place in a Healthy Relationship

I (Adonis) am speaking from the male perspective here, but I'm sure there are women who have dabbled in pornography as well. If you are a woman who has struggled with this, keep reading.

Chances are, almost every guy has either looked at porn or have been tempted to look at it at least once in his life. In junior high, I remember finding some of my dad's porn movies and secretly watching them. Though that was many years ago, I can still remember some of those images so vividly in my mind. That's the power of porn and the effect that it has on you.

Porn is one of those activities that is definitely outside the boundaries of a healthy relationship. It's all about creating a fantasy world of how intimacy is supposed to be, look, and even sound like. It builds an expectation in your mind and creates an unsatisfying lust.

There's almost no chance of you having a healthy dating relationship if porn is also a part of your world. It drives you to imagine yourself doing those same sex acts with your girlfriend in your mind. Before you know it, you masturbate as you imagine you and her together. Then, when you and her are in any type of intimate setting alone, it will be harder for you to have self-control.

Here's a scenario for any guy who may have a secret porn addiction. Let's say you're in a relationship but she doesn't know you look at porn. She's saving herself for her husband and you respect her for that. Fast-forward two years down the road and you two get married. It's the wedding night and your first sexual encounter with her. Your expectation will be for her to perform like the ladies in the porn movies you've been watching and that will cause major problems for the both of you.

You may feel like your sexual needs are not being met and you might begin to look for that pleasure outside of your marriage covenant. She, on the other hand, may feel devalued by your gestures and requests of sexual acts and positions. What she looked at as beautiful has now become something that makes her feel like your prostitute. Bottom line—ditch the porn.

1. Truly be repentant in your heart and receive God's grace and forgiveness.

His love for you hasn't changed and it continues to run deeper than any mistake you can make. He loves you no matter what and is always there to help you. If you've fallen, then it's time to get back up and keep moving forward. Learn from the mistake you made and seek to set up safeguards and boundaries that will prevent you from making the same mistake again.

There are many well-meaning Christian couples that make the mistake of having sex outside of marriage. It doesn't mean you are a liar or hypocrite. It also doesn't mean that you don't love God. It means you are human and made a mistake just like many heroes in the Bible. It's what you do after that mistake that determines how successful the relationship can or will be.

2. Reach out to your accountability partner.

This is usually easier said than done. Our human nature is to cover up the wrong doings in our lives for fear of our weaknesses and mistakes being exposed. You must remember that your accountability partner is for you and not against you. This is the person that you have chosen to help lead and guide you on your relationship journey. They are there to offer encouragement, support, and guidance on your way to getting the relationship back on track.

If they are a true accountability partner, then they will keep anything you share with them with the utmost confidentiality. You must be true to your commitment to them, as well, and give them the right to check in on your relationship without you feeling like they are overstepping the boundaries.

If you really want them to be your accountability partner,

then you must respect their advice and input without being offended. Remember, they are there to help you avoid making the same mistake twice.

3. Make a brand-new commitment to sexual purity.

Making this commitment could mean that some of your former activities might need to change. For instance, you both might need to sit down and truthfully examine and talk about some of the actions that led up to the sexual mistake. Once you identify those actions or activities, you must consciously avoid those from this point forward in order to remain sexually pure in your relationship.

So many people make the mistake of entering back into those same actions, thinking that they will be strong enough this time to not go all the way. They only end up deceiving themselves and eventually end up in mistake number two and so on and so on. The cycle repeats until eventually there is no effort at all to abstain from sexual contact. In other words, it becomes out of control.

A Little Prayer for God's Help with Sexual Purity

Dear God, I am hurting from past mistakes of sexual sin and I need Your help to stop the pain. I acknowledge that what I've done and what I'm doing is not working for me. I invite You into my heart and life from this moment on to help me with this. I want to know Your ways and follow Your ways starting right now. I thank You for Your forgiveness and love toward me. Give me strength to follow You and walk in agreement with what the Bible says about sexual purity. Amen

Inappropriate Conversations

"I love it when you talk dirty to me."

This is an area that should be off-limits in the dating relationship, as well as sharing risqué pictures with each other. Sexual conversations and little innuendos alluding to sexual acts have the power and potential to take you to places you don't mean to be. These conversations create images in your mind and stir up your passion for one another. It will cause you to think about sex and even envision yourselves having sex together. Make no mistake about it; whatever happens in your mind will happen in time.

If there are any sexual comments or inappropriate talk coming from the person you are dating, please use caution because that could be a potential red flag. You will easily be able to tell if that was a one-time joking comment or something more. If that type of talk continues, they are trying to get you to bite the bait. And if you're the one doing the baiting, know that you're engaging in risky behavior.

Here's a hypothetical scenario. Let's say Lisa and John have been out three times now. On the last date, Lisa was caught off guard by what appeared to be an inappropriate comment made by John. They were joking around and he alluded to couples engaging in a very loose sexual act. He said it in a joking manner and Lisa even laughed along, but later on that night it bothered her.

Lisa has a choice to make. She can either kindly explain to John how those comments make her feel or she could just not mention anything and hope that he doesn't make any more.

Here's the problem with her not saying anything to John: When John made the comment, he noticed Lisa laughed at it. In his mind, he immediately thought that she was okay with this kind of talk and he just might continue those comments to see how far he can go.

To keep sex completely out of a relationship is no easy task, especially when you are attracted to each other. There is a saying that sex ends at marriage. Why not try ending sex in dating and starting it in marriage?

Oral Sex: "I did not have sex with that woman."

"Is oral sex crossing a line?"

"Is it really sex?"

"It's okay as long there is no actual intercourse . . . right?"

This is a topic that comes with many perspectives and opinions. Hollywood and porn stars have given a very twisted and perverted perception of oral sex. Bill Clinton once stated, "I did not have sex with that woman." That statement was definitely based on his interpretation of sexual intercourse versus oral sex.

In the pursuit of trying to date without crossing a line and entering into premarital sex, your principles, deal-breakers, and values can sometimes become very twisted when in the heat of the moment. Oral sex becomes lost in the gray area of relationships and not many people, especially pastors, want to talk about it.

Some couples that are caught up in the moment of their hormones being out of control during a make-out session will be tempted to use oral sex as a way of fulfillment or release with the idea that they are not having real sex, so it's not going against their morals or God's Word. To their surprise, they still feel guilty after the act, but once they cross that line, it's a downward spiral from there. It may bring about a certain amount of pleasure in the moment, but also may bring a certain amount of strain and problems in the relationship. Then it becomes easy to justify having premarital sex since you've already gone that far.

I can't really prove this statistic but I can take a wild guess and say that 90 percent of men either have already engaged in oral sex or would like to have it one day. When a guy is given the opportunity, it is going to be very hard for him to turn the offer down, even if he is a godly man and trying to date the right way. Once again, it is better to stay away from potential situations that could lead to any form of sexual activity.

Ladies, don't feel like that's a way to keep him or to make him yours. And men, this is not the way to a woman's heart in a dating relationship. You must treat her like a lady that you would want to marry one day and fight for the purity in the relationship.

Oral sex is a very powerful, intimate act that has the power and potential to bind people together and even create soul ties. You are exposing each other to very intimate parts of your anatomy and still engaging in a very real sexual act. It may even cause you to look at one another differently from that moment on.

So remember, oral sex, as well as sexual intercourse, belong within the marriage covenant between husband and wife.

THE STORY OF SAMSON AND DELILAH:

Baggage and Soul Ties

Whether you are a Christian or not, chances are you have heard the story of Samson and Delilah. Samson was a man of God with supernatural strength who fell victim to sexual immorality. He could not control his own desires even though he had great physical strength. His lack of self-control led him to a series of bad choices and decisions, which brought detrimental consequences to his life.

Many preachers speak from this story to give warning about sexual immorality and what it has the potential to lead to. In youth groups, it's the first story that's always talked about when the topic on dating or sex is being discussed. In most cases, it produces a fear mentality instead of a "Why did this happen?" mentality. I think it's important to have a clear understanding of why and how it happened so it will educate and equip people to avoid the mistakes, pitfalls, and potential detours of destiny.

When Heather and I began research for our "Dating God's Way" class and for this book, I began to look at the entire story of Samson and Delilah with a different perspective. Several questions drove me to dive deeper into his life. What would cause a man to stay with a woman who he knows is trying to get him killed? Why is he continually making the same mistake over and over? Doesn't he know this is wrong? Why can't he control himself? Why isn't his strength enough to stop this? Upon further review, I realized this is a story made up of disregarded deal-breakers, unseen baggage, and unbroken soul ties.

I'll give an overview and briefly discuss my opinion of the story, but you are always welcome to read the story at full length in the Bible in the Book of Judges, chapters fourteen, fifteen, and sixteen. Now, let me warn you, this may be a totally different perspective about this story than you've ever heard, but I'm merely trying to provoke some thought behind Samson's actions.

When Samson saw the woman he wanted for a wife, he immediately told his parents and asked them to get her for him as his wife (apparently, that's how it worked in those days). The Bible makes no mention of them having sex before marriage.

Long story short, his new wife betrayed him and told her family a secret between the two of them. This little incident started a domino effect of bad choices. In his anger, Samson went off to fight the Philistines. In Samson's absence, his father-in-law gave Samson's wife to the best man at his wedding because he thought Samson was so mad at her and would never want to have anything to do with her again.

When Samson found out his wife was given to his best man, you can imagine how furious he was. Enraged, he went off to continue fighting with the Philistines. I'll fast forward a little here, but Samson's wife (who now belonged to his best friend) was eventually killed by her own people (the Philistines) because of all the grief Samson was causing them.

Fast forward again. Samson has sex with a prostitute. Then later he ends up falling in love with a woman named Delilah. His enemies approach Delilah behind Samson's back and promise her money if she can find out the secret to Samson's strength. She constantly pesters him day and night until he reveals the secret.

> "She kept at it day after day, nagging and
> tormenting him. Finally, he was fed up—
> he couldn't take another minute of it. He spilled it.
> He told her, 'A razor has never touched my head.
> I've been God's Nazirite from conception.
> If I were shaved, my strength would leave me;
> I would be as helpless as any other mortal.'"
> (Judges 16:16–17 MSG)

His actions, decisions, and disobedience to God eventually lead to his capture and death.

Now, let's reflect back on these previous circumstances and get an understanding of the possible condition of Samson's heart, soul, and thought process. Here are a few insights I would like to share with you from a different perspective. Please keep in mind, I am not condoning what Samson did, nor am I in agreement with his actions. I am simply trying to take a look at the reasons these actions may have come about.

1. The person who he thought was the right one for him ended up betraying his trust. To make matters worse, she ended up married to his best friend and was eventually killed by her own people.

> "But Samson said to his father, 'Get her for me.
> She's the one I want—she's the right one.'"
> (Judges 14:3 MSG)

Try to put yourself in Samson's sandals for a moment. You can only imagine how Samson must have felt. His wife betrayed him, ended up with his best friend without his knowledge, and was now dead without him ever having a chance to talk with her about it. Now he's heartbroken, frustrated, angry, and confused all at the same time. He never actually got closure from any of this, and is no doubt carrying around baggage from a relationship he viewed as a failure. He will probably have a hard time trusting a woman again. His heart is probably hardened toward true love and he's probably questioning if it is even worth it to try again.

2. His moral compass gets thrown off track and now he doesn't hesitate to engage in premarital sex. He went from thinking of marriage and commitment (like when he saw his first wife) to only thinking of instant gratification when he saw the prostitute.

> "Samson went to Gaza and saw a prostitute.
> He went to her . . ."
> (Judges 16:1 MSG)

Obviously, he is not thinking straight at all. He's probably so emotionally unstable that he's looking for something or someone to make the pain go away.

3. He ends up falling in love with a woman named Delilah. I want to point out that the Bible clearly states he was in love with her.

> "Some time later Samson fell in love with
> a woman named Delilah . . ."
> (Judges 16:4 NLT)

Take note, his heart was in love but wasn't completely healed from his failed marriage. He probably thought, "I need to take this one for a test-drive first before I make the huge commitment of marriage again." Or maybe he thought, "I don't ever want to get married again; that was a horrible experience." Whatever it was, this type of thinking no doubt led to living together and premarital sex.

Samson also had some huge distrust issues going on in this new relationship. Delilah kept asking him for the secret to his strength and he kept giving her false answers. In all reality, he should never have told her the secret but in that moment I'm sure he was still holding on to a little unforgiveness toward his first wife. He probably was thinking, "The last time I shared a secret with someone I loved, they totally betrayed my trust and I will never do that again."

> "She said, 'How can you say "I love you" when
> you won't even trust me? Three times now you've

toyed with me, like a cat with a mouse,
refusing to tell me the secret of your great strength.'"
(Judges 16:15 MSG)

4. He stayed in a relationship with a woman he knew was trying to get him captured and killed by his enemies.

Siren alert . . . this is a huge deal-breaker! You should not be in a relationship with someone who is trying to get you killed. You're probably thinking, "Well, that's obvious." But Samson couldn't see this because he had on emotional blinders. Every time he would give her the wrong answer about his strength, she would do to him exactly as he said. That should have been an indicator to Samson that it was time to exit the relationship.

Unfortunately, he couldn't because of the strong soul ties that were formed between he and Delilah. His mind could have been trying to tell him the truth about Delilah but his heart and emotions were too tangled with hers. Or maybe he kept giving her chances thinking that she would be loyal and restore his trust in women.

The truth is that we don't know exactly what was going through Samson's mind but we can probably agree that he wasn't thinking straight. We can read the story today and clearly see the pitfalls and mistakes. But, like Samson, when you are in the moment and outside of the boundaries of God's Word you can easily become oblivious to reality or the danger you are in. It may not be the danger of losing your life, but it could be the dangers of heartache, wounded emotions, or missing your destiny all because of a wrong relationship.

So What Exactly Causes a Soul Tie?

A soul tie is supposed to be a spiritual and emotional bond that is formed between a husband and a wife. There is nothing that can prepare you for what a soul tie feels like—both for how wonderful it is in the boundaries of marriage, and how difficult it can be to overcome when a relationship ends.

One-night stands and friends with benefits can also cause emotional damage. They, too, create soul ties. Others have gone down the path of promiscuity. Some do it because of a lack of confidence. You may feel better for a day, but when the person leaves you the next day, next week, or next month what do you think that does for your confidence?

It is important for you both to have the same belief when it comes to sexual purity. We are all human; we all have moments of weakness. If you date someone who doesn't have the same belief as you, you are looking for trouble. As much as you want to stand your ground, you will eventually break if continuously pushed.

When you both have the same belief, there is someone to remain strong while the other is weak: "Two are stronger than one" (Ecclesiastes 4:9). I was once told, "Why sacrifice a lifetime for a moment?" That really stuck with me because a sexual act is in the moment and that one act has the potential to mess up your future marriage or even, in some cases, cause you a lifetime worth of emotional damage.

DON'T CARRY SOMEONE ELSE'S BAGGAGE WHEN ALL YOU HAVE IS A CARRY-ON

If you are human, you have baggage. According to Merriam-Webster, baggage is defined as "intangible things (as feelings, circumstances, or beliefs) that get in the way." It can also be defined as past experiences or long-held ideas regarded as burdens and impediments.

The first definition refers to things that get in the way. That is exactly what will happen when you bring baggage into a relationship; it will get in the way! So, if everyone has baggage, how do you not bring it into a relationship?

> "Then Jesus said, 'Come to me, all of you who
> are weary and carry heavy burdens,
> and I will give you rest.'" (Matthew 11:28 NLT)

It's easier said than done, but the truth is God doesn't want you to carry any burdens, much less someone else's burdens that you weren't meant to carry. Adonis says it this way: "Gentlemen, you don't want to end up being a bell hop."

When you enter a relationship, you don't want to carry any past hurts or disappointments into it, just as you wouldn't want the person you are dating to show up on your doorstep with their baggage. If that happens, pretty soon you'll end up on an episode of *Hoarders*! In order to limit your baggage, you have to deal with your past experiences before getting into a new relationship.

Some of your past experiences may come up in your new relationship. Just make sure those past experiences are just that— experiences, not baggage. You don't have to share every single experience with the person you are dating. Of course, you don't need to hide things either, but it's probably not a good idea to talk about all your past sexual relationships or past failed relationships. Before you share, ask yourself, "Do they really need to know that about me and my past?" If the answer is no, then don't share. If the answer is yes, then let it come out naturally and probably not with every single detail.

If you are both carrying baggage, that makes it hard to focus on the relationship. It gets in the way and can cause hurt and disunity between the two of you. A lot of us have the tendency to want to help and pick up someone else's baggage, but all that does is cause you to get hurt. Don't throw your back out carrying someone else's baggage.

Baggage of Divorce

For me (Heather), my divorce could have been baggage. It was a failed relationship and I could have taken that failure into my next relationship or worse, into my next marriage. I couldn't erase the fact that I was married before, but I could take responsibility for my actions, ask for forgiveness, and move forward knowing I could make different choices.

You need to free yourself from the baggage of failure in general. If you take that failure mindset into your next relationship, you may unknowingly put a wall up. You may think you failed once and you don't want to fail again, so you make adjustments based on that failure, but you don't want to be motivated by that fear.

In my case, I asked God to show me how to heal from failure. I said, "I messed up and I'm going to take full responsibility for it." I asked God to show me the errors of my ways. It was then that God started to show me what I had done wrong and the hurts that I had caused my ex-husband.

During that time, I would call my ex-husband when God would reveal something to me and let him know how sorry I was for hurting him during our marriage. My ex-husband was very forgiving and even though our relationship was over, it was very good for me to ask for forgiveness and let him know I did things wrong in our relationship. More importantly, I needed to take responsibility for those things.

Though we truly did have a friendship, my ex and I both decided that it wouldn't be fair to our future spouses to remain friends. Not long after we ended our friendship, I met Adonis. Through watching God change me and my life, my ex-husband started going to church, got saved, and that is where he met his wife. How is that for a story of God turning something painful into something glorious?

My divorce was no longer baggage. If you are divorced, yours doesn't have to be either.

Are Children Baggage?

Sometimes people consider children to be baggage. They definitely are not. Children are a blessing from God. However, if you know that you would look at them as baggage and wouldn't be able to love them as your own, then don't date someone with children.

If there is baggage associated with children, it usually is in the form of the children's other parent, whether that be an ex-husband or ex-wife. If you are dating someone who has children and they still have a rough relationship with their ex, that is baggage. If they are constantly fighting over or about the children, that is baggage. You will definitely feel the weight of that baggage in your relationship. If they have good communication with their ex or no communication other than what is necessary, then it's not baggage.

Financial Baggage

What about financial baggage? Should you wait to date until you are debt free? Should you not date someone in debt? Let's look at what is baggage and what is not.

- Do you continuously spend more than you have?
- Are you losing sleep at night because you can't pay your bills?
- Are debt collectors calling you nonstop?
- Is your bank account in the red?

If you answered yes to any of the above questions, then I will give you some great advice. You need to put down this book right now and pick up a Dave Ramsey book! If I haven't lost you, then ask yourself these questions:

- Have I filed bankruptcy, but have been able to sustain since?
- Do I have credit card debt, but am working to pay it off?
- Do I have student loans, but can pay my monthly payments?

If you answered yes to any of these questions, then you probably don't have financial baggage as long as you continue to be responsible. Financial baggage can be a big one because if your relationship moves to marriage then you automatically take on your spouse's financial baggage.

Finances are one of the leading problems in marriages, so why would you want to start your marriage off with financial problems? Concentrate on paying off your debt so you can concentrate on your new relationship when you're ready.

Baggage of a Broken Heart

Women and men deal with breakups differently. While women are usually better about sharing their feelings with others and finding ways to stay preoccupied, guys aren't so great at this.

Guys get broken hearts, whether we like to admit it or not. That usually causes us as men to build up a wall around us to ensure that we are never hurt in that manner again. This causes problems because now we have the potential to see every woman as a threat against our manhood. It causes us to self-sabotage a potentially great relationship in fear of being broken-hearted once again.

Generational Baggage

You may not even realize it, but you may be carrying baggage from your upbringing. This is especially true if your parents have divorced.

Have you healed from the hurt of your parents' divorce? What if you saw your dad cheat on your mom? Maybe you're suspicious of everyone you date. Maybe you expect the person you are dating to cheat on you.

You may not even realize that you are carrying around that baggage. Stop and ask yourself those questions. If you have siblings, it may be a good idea to look at their relationships too. If they struggle with their relationships in the same way you do, then that may be a good indicator that it is something from your upbringing. Talk with them about it and see if that helps you all to bring the issue to light, so you can heal from it.

Both my brother and I (Heather) struggled with our relationships. As a matter of fact, we had the exact same patterns. We would date someone for a year or two and that's it. Most people would look at him and think he's unable to commit, but most would look at me and think I haven't found the right one. In reality, we both had the same issue. It was a pattern caused by our upbringing.

Family baggage can be deep-seeded, like when Adonis's dad told him to never get married or have kids. After you have healed from it and given it to God, it is so important to get around couples that have healthy relationships so you have a model.

Emotional Baggage: Insecurity and a Bad Self-Image

One of the most unattractive things is insecurity. If you are carrying around this piece of baggage, it's almost like you have one of those big red circles with the line through it around you, telling everyone around you that you're off limits.

As I've become a parent, I've heard numerous times that the best thing you can do for your children is to have a healthy relationship with your spouse. That healthy relationship gives your children security and confidence. Security starts at a young age, as does insecurity. You may not have had that security with your parents, but you do have that security with your Heavenly Father.

I always carried the baggage of bad self-image. This goes back to my childhood and is even generational in my family. My grandma is a fat-o-phobe, if there can be such a thing. In other words, my grandma doesn't like people to be fat, especially her children and grandchildren. If you were overweight, my grandma would let you know.

It affected my mom growing up. My mom wasn't a fat-o-phobe, but she didn't want me to struggle with weight and I was a chunky kid. I wasn't obese, but just chunky enough to get picked on a little. Keep in mind, those were the days when kids played outside a lot and most kids looked like beanpoles. I looked more like a bean.

My mom put me in Weight Watchers at a very young age and had me try a few other diets as I grew up. I know she was just trying to help, but that, combined with getting picked on and not being as small as everyone else, caused me to have a bad self-image.

The most I ever weighed in high school was 133 pounds at

5'4", but the fact that I know that says a lot about how much I obsessed about my weight. This was baggage and I took it into all of my relationships, even after I lost fifteen pounds after high school. I was always asking myself if I was thin enough. I even carried it into my first marriage. I thought I had laid that baggage down, but I picked it right back up. It didn't matter how much weight I lost or how much I exercised, I still felt overweight.

I finally realized that I am created in God's image and that it's more important to be healthy than a particular size. It wouldn't have been fair to Adonis to bring that baggage into our relationship and assume that he's not attracted to me because I'm not thin enough.

Do I sometimes still struggle? Absolutely, because being thin is all over this world, but I don't let that affect my relationship with Adonis. When I do struggle, I stop and ask God to help me see myself the way He sees me.

> "The Lord is my rock, and my safe place,
> and the One Who takes me out of trouble. My God
> is my rock, in Whom I am safe. He is my safe-
> covering, my saving strength, and my strong tower."
> (Psalm 18:2 NLV)

There are millions of reasons to be insecure, especially in today's society. The main thing you have to focus on is that no matter the reason for your struggle with insecurity, you can find your identity in Christ.

> "No power in the sky above or in the earth below—
> indeed, nothing in all creation will ever be able to
> separate us from the love of God that is revealed in
> Christ Jesus our Lord." (Romans 8:39 NLT)

You can lay down one piece of baggage only to walk down the street and pick up another. Until you find your identity in Christ, there will always be opportunity to make you feel insecure. To be attractive to someone else, you have to find your confidence, just as you wouldn't be attracted to someone without confidence. Confidence is very attractive, but don't confuse confidence with arrogance.

If you're already in a relationship, then practice helping build each other up. It's not healthy to find your identity in each other, but it certainly doesn't hurt to help each other's confidence.

Emotional Baggage: Abandonment

You can carry the baggage of abandonment for years. You may even be carrying a fear that the person you are in a relationship with is going to leave you. This may go back to one or both of your parents leaving you (like Adonis's dad) or maybe everyone you get into a relationship with really does leave you. If this happens, you may not be putting yourself completely out there in relationships or fully engaging emotionally. When you don't open yourself up, a relationship cannot survive.

You can be free from abandonment. It may not happen overnight, but it has to start with a choice to want to be free from this baggage. Once you've made that decision, you have to ask God to walk it out with you. The one thing you can always rely on is that God will never abandon you.

Emotional Baggage: Selfishness

I (Heather) was very selfish, especially when it came to relationships. I'm not sure why; maybe it was because I was the baby in the family and my grandparents gave me extra love and attention. Or maybe it was because my mom spoiled me.

Either way, it wasn't until I met God that I realized how selfish I was. I had been blinded by the fact that I was a nice person; I was both kind and compassionate. I wasn't ever mean to anyone, but I did what I wanted to do. That was part of the reason all of my past relationships failed. Once they stopped being fun for me, I would move on. I never pressed through any relationships because I thought I didn't have to. I would just move on and find someone else who made me happy.

Back then, it was all about me and my feelings. If I took that same selfish attitude into my relationship with Adonis, it surely would have ended the way all my other relationships did. Selfishness isn't a personality trait—it's baggage. I had to lay that baggage down before God and thank God that I did because once we had children, selfishness had no room in our house!

Sexual Baggage: The Ghosts of Past Relationships

Hurt from past relationships can be a huge source of baggage. This is especially true when there has been a past sexual relationship. A sexual relationship creates soul ties that make it hard to break away. They're a lot more powerful than we give credit for. After all, God created sex as the only time a man and woman can physically be one.

How do you break a soul tie that has been established? Start with asking God to help you sever the tie. Then, ask yourself how you got there in the first place. If necessary, forgive yourself and put guardrails in place to avoid making the same mistake.

There are also some practical things you can do; like avoiding your ex until you are fully healed, or maybe even avoiding them completely. Delete all contact information and pictures. It may also help to get rid of any items in your house that remind you of your ex.

It's very important to not blame the next person you get into a relationship with for the hurt the person in the previous relationship caused. If your boyfriend or girlfriend ended the relationship and gave you no explanation or closure, you have to learn how to move forward with the ability to trust again. If someone cheated on you, don't assume the next person is going to cheat on you. When you do that, you are setting your relationship up for failure. It is impossible to establish trust if you're already going in distrusting before you even get to know them.

How fair would it be to you if someone entered a relationship with you already thinking you may cheat, on them, lie to them, or treat them badly? It's important to go into a relationship with a clean slate. It's not fair to you or the other person when you don't.

If your relationship ended due to cheating, and you were the one who cheated, go back and figure out why you cheated. You may want to spend extra time on chapter 11 about sexual purity. You must be honest with yourself, and sometimes that is very difficult. Cheating is a selfish act no matter how you look at it. Determine how you got into the situation and how you can prevent being in that place in the future. It's also important to ask for forgiveness and to forgive yourself.

If you were the one cheated on, you first have to forgive the person who cheated on you. I know firsthand it's not that easy to do. But if you don't forgive your ex, you will carry that baggage with you wherever you go.

"Look after each other so that none of you fails
to receive the grace of God. Watch out that no
poisonous root of bitterness grows up to trouble you,
corrupting many." (Hebrews 12:15 NLT)

Sexual Baggage: Past Sexual Abuse

Fortunately for me, I (Heather) have not dealt with this myself. However, in my line of work, I have seen and heard about many horrible, unspeakable things. While I am not a licensed counselor, I can tell you this: Do not live in fear or shame. No one should ever have to endure sexual abuse, or the aftermath of emotions, but there is freedom from this baggage too. God can provide this freedom if you let Him. There are people out there available for counseling specifically in this area. Don't be afraid to reach out and get the help you need.

Anger Toward God

Maybe you carry anger toward God for not coming through for you in your past relationships. Or maybe you have been believing for your spouse and you feel that God hasn't come through with His promise. Maybe you're mad because life hasn't turned out the way you'd envisioned.

If your past relationship failed, then it's because God closed the door. If you don't see your breakup as a good thing now, you will. What's important is that you chalk it up to experience and learn from it.

If you've been waiting for your special someone, I assure you he or she is out there. Start putting these things into practice, make the necessary changes, and continue to draw close to God. Wouldn't you rather be in the right relationship than the wrong one?

"Give all your worries and cares to God,
for he cares about you." (1 Peter 5:7 NLT)

In order to move ahead, first identify any areas of baggage you
may be carrying.

- Are you struggling with an addiction?
- Have you not healed from your past relationship hurts?
- Have you not forgiven yourself for past mistakes?
- Have you not forgiven others?
- Are you angry?
- Do you carry bitterness?
- Do you struggle with insecurity?
- Are you carrying the baggage of failure?
- Do you struggle in your finances?

Second, you have to lay that baggage down.

- Give God the burdens you carry.
- Let God heal you.
- Forgive yourself.
- Make amends with others, if possible.
- Recognize when you try to pick that baggage back up.

Lastly, do not carry someone else's baggage. It wasn't meant
for you to carry! Their baggage may seem light at first, but it won't
be if you carry it long enough.

Priorities: Is the person you are dating a priority?

A dating relationship is the practice run for marriage. You may not be ready to get married now, but a dating relationship is great practice for it, no matter how far away from marriage you are.

If you aren't willing to make the relationship—and the person you're in a relationship with—a priority, then maybe you shouldn't be dating now anyway.

Ways to make them a priority:

- Don't choose everything else over them.
- Set aside time specifically for them.
- Occasionally text or call to let them know you care.
- Include them in your life's decision-making processes. People you are dating want to feel like they are contributing to your well being.

CAN WE JUST BE FRIENDS?

The Danger of Having Close Friends of the Opposite Sex

I (Heather) used to be the person who would argue that men and women can absolutely be friends. I always had close guy friends growing up and as a young adult. Even after I got saved, I was still arguing that it was okay. Boy, have my opinions changed.

I can't give you scripture, because the fact is nowhere in the Bible does it say men and women can't be friends. What I can do is share some of my experiences with you and challenge you to evaluate any relationships you have with others of the opposite sex.

One day I heard God say that I needed to prepare for my marriage and, in doing so, I needed to evaluate my friendships with the opposite sex. I thought I'd look at them, but my opinion was not going to change. If there was a club for opposite-sex friendships, I would have been the president, vice president, secretary, and treasurer!

A Last-Minute Marriage Confession

After I graduated college and left my home state of Wisconsin, I kept in contact with a lot of my male friends from high school, previous coworkers, and even some old boyfriends. Most of them I had lengthy friendships with.

After God spoke that word to me, I planned a trip back to WI for my friend's wedding. It was a male friend who had been a coworker. We didn't talk every day, but had remained in contact throughout the years.

This was also the trip when I was going to share with everyone that I was getting divorced.

I was out with my girlfriends the night before the wedding, and we ran into my friend; he was so excited that I was there for his wedding. After talking for a while, I shared with him that I was getting divorced. Instead of showing some type of sympathy, he looked at me and said, "I wish I would have known. Why didn't you tell me sooner? If I would have known, I wouldn't be getting married tomorrow!"

What? Where did that come from? This was someone who I thought was just a friend and all of a sudden he is professing his love for me—the night before his wedding!

The next day I sat at his wedding knowing what he had said to me the night before. It weighed heavily on me. Not only had he shared it with me, but he also shared it with one of his groomsmen. I went from feeling like I was there to celebrate my friend to feeling like I could break up his marriage before it even started.

I felt ashamed, like I no longer belonged there. What if she had found out? This was supposed to be the happiest day of her life and I may ruin it.

All along I thought we were just friends, but the honest truth was that he wanted more than friendship. How was I supposed to know if he never expressed that to me? How could I have been so blind? Was I being blind with my other friendships? That made me stop and take a look at those male friendships. Did they feel the same way too?

Friends Since High School

I had one friend in particular who I had been friends with since I was in high school. I thought there was no way something like this would happen with him, so I came right out and asked him about our friendship and what it meant to him. Big mistake! He, too, unleashed a truth that was I wasn't prepared to hear: He was waiting and looking for his "Heather."

He said he didn't know if he would ever meet someone quite like me. He had spent his twenties and thirties single or in and out of relationships because he was comparing other women to me— and we had never dated.

I knew it was time for me to give up these friendships. But the truth was, I liked the male attention. The more I thought about it, the more selfish it seemed. These friendships weren't nearly as important as a husband or future husband, so I severed all of my relationships with my guy friends. To be honest, some of them were hard to sever because I had known them so long.

I sat down one day and typed up an e-mail to my guy friends and just explained my heart, and that God was preparing me for my future marriage. I know this must have floored some of them since I hadn't been walking with God most of my life. To this day, I don't know what's happened to most of them, but I hope that I set a good example for them and their future relationships.

By the time I started dating Adonis, my belief had changed and I continued to sever those relationships with my guy friends. Adonis, however, did not share my new belief.

The Love Triangle

When Adonis and I started dating, he had a female friend. Before we started hanging out, every now and then I would see them hanging out together. Initially, I even thought they were dating—and I wasn't alone. A mutual friend assured me that she and Adonis were not dating, so I proceeded to spend time with him. I did not want to step on anyone's toes or interfere in anyone's relationship.

To be certain, I asked Adonis about her and he assured me that they were just friends. It was the perfect opportunity for me to share my revelation about what God had shown me about friendships. I thought it was interesting how God had shown me how important that was going to be for my next relationship. I also thought, surely, God would have gone before me and prepared his heart the same way so the next man I date wouldn't have any female friends. That wasn't the case.

Weeks later, I was at work and someone overheard me telling one of my girlfriends that I'd been going golfing with one of my pastors. This person then tells me that Adonis is already seeing someone else, his female friend, that he has already met her parents, and that she believes Adonis is going to be her husband. Can you believe it? I can.

I immediately called Adonis and told him we needed to talk. We met and I told him what had happened. I asked Adonis if he had met her parents and he said that he had; he had been introduced to them at church, along with several other people. I asked him if he knew that she thought he was her future husband, and by the look on his face, I knew he was shocked. Here Adonis was, in a relationship that he thought was a friendship but all along she was hoping for something more.

Not only did this friendship give a bad perception (like my male friendships had), but it was also something that he brought into our relationship that we had to work through. That's not something that you want to deal with at the beginning of a relationship.

I questioned if he was being truthful with me. Luckily, I knew from his reaction and our conversation that he really wasn't seeing her. But now, since we all knew each other, there was an awkward situation—and it could have been avoided.

If you are in friendships with members of the opposite sex right now, ask them what their feelings are for you. Awkward, yes, but not as awkward as you starting to date someone and then they profess their love to you. They may not be honest with you. Sometimes people are embarrassed to share their feelings or may fear rejection, but at least you tried. But that doesn't stop you from being honest with them.

If you are hanging out with someone to determine if you want to pursue a dating relationship, do yourself and them a favor by being honest. If you know a friend is interested in you but you don't feel the same way, don't try to maintain the friendship just because you don't want to hurt them. On the other side, don't hang around waiting for someone to take you out of the friend zone because you may end up getting hurt when your friend starts dating someone else.

Lessons in Love

A friendship can give the outward appearance that there is something more there. When you are continuously hanging out with someone, people take notice. Even if both of your intentions are nothing more than to just be friends, you can be closing the door to an actual dating prospect. That prospect doesn't want to compete with someone else for your attention and may not even look twice at you because it seems you are already dating someone. In other words, you can be closing both your door and your friend's door to finding someone.

Another misconception some of us have is that a relationship that starts out as friendship may turn into something stronger. We all want that—the foundation of a good relationship is friendship. Can you have a friend from high school or college you reconnect with and then end up in a relationship? Absolutely! Can you hang out with someone as friends while you are trying to get to know each other to determine whether or not you are interested? Yes, that is exactly what you are supposed to do. You should be friends first. It's the point at which you know there is nothing more than a friendship there, or you suspect they may have more than feelings of friendship for you and you don't feel the same, that you enter the danger zone.

When you are hanging out with someone, you know if there's chemistry or an attraction. It's possible that you can be friends

142

with someone for a long time and then magic happens, just like in the movies. That is possible, but the reality is that you typically are attracted or not attracted to someone once you get to know them, and that doesn't always change. This isn't a hard and fast rule I'm trying to set here. All I'm trying to get you to do is evaluate your friendships.

Do your friendships fall into this definition? Do you want more than a friendship with someone? If you do, put this book down right now and go tell them! The worst that can happen is they reject you and you lose a friend. Even so, that's not the end of the world.

If you don't have feelings other than friendship, are you in the friendship because you like the attention from someone of the opposite sex? The truth is, God made us to be in relationship with the opposite sex. God gave Adam a helpmate: Eve! It's normal to want that, but at what point is it a friendship out of selfish, feel-good motives or a hidden agenda? Is that friendship blocking you from meeting your future mate? Are you blocking your friend from meeting their future mate?

Transitioning from Friends to Dating

Someone at one time or another has said to you that the key to a great relationship is a friendship. That is true.

I (Heather) know I just went through a million reasons why you shouldn't be casual friends with someone of the opposite sex. So, let's talk about transitioning from a friendship into a relationship, and what practical dating looks like.

You are most likely going to do one of two things: You're either going to intentionally go out on a date with someone, knowing that you are *already* interested in that person or you're going to go on a date with someone to see if you *could be* interested or if you two have enough in common to date.

In either case, you could go out on that first date to find out that you definitely aren't interested and it ends there. There are other times when you really enjoy your first date and decide to go out on a second or third. Once you get to know each other a little better, you decide some of your foundational beliefs don't match up. In that case, you enjoy hanging out with that person, but know that isn't the person for you based on the foundational things.

If you decided they aren't for you and maintain that relationship without being honest, you are leading them on. Even if you talk about it and you say, "We're just friends. We're cool right?" Well, what is the other person going to say, "No, I really like you"? When you put them in that situation, most likely they are going to hide or suppress their feelings for you in the hopes one day you will change your mind. Most of the time, people don't change their mind. Can it happen? Anything can happen, but why put yourself in that situation?

If you start a genuine friendship, it can be hard to break away because you like hanging out with that person. The best advice in that situation is to be able to say, "I'm not helping them find their spouse and it's not helping me find my spouse." Just because you aren't looking for your spouse, it doesn't mean they aren't. As soon as you know the relationship isn't going anywhere, the best thing to do is to be honest.

I know that it's hard because we don't want to hurt people, nor do we like feeling rejected, but rejection is usually protection. You have to look at it like the longer you spend with that person, the longer you spend trying to find your spouse. Don't let that friendship be what's holding you back. Remember, you could be holding them back too.

Let's Just Be Friends

If you're on the receiving end of the "just friends" conversation, what they are saying is "I don't want to pursue a relationship with you," or "I like the attention you are giving me or how you make me feel, but you are not for me."

If someone says they want to hang out as friends and see where it goes, that's completely different. In that case, they are

---

Heather's Big List of Dating No's

- Don't be driven by emotions.
- Don't ignore red flags or deal-breakers.
- Don't over-spiritualize.
- Don't force something that isn't there.
- Don't have close friendships with the opposite sex when you know it's not going anywhere.

Don't Do This on a First Date:

- Don't talk about an ex.
- Don't use your cell phone or text unnecessarily.
- Don't name drop.
- Don't talk about money.

---

saying they would like to get to know you better to see if there could potentially be a relationship in the future. If it takes a long friendship to see if you like each other, then so be it. You are committed to that person to see if you like them. That *doesn't* mean you are in ten friendships looking to see which one you are interested in. You aren't on ABC's *The Bachelor*.

"THE ONE"

God, Is This the Right Person for Me?

How do you know? When do you know? What is knowing suppose to feel like?

One of my pastor friends says it like this: "Whoever you marry, that's the right person for you." You might say, "But what if I marry an idiot?" Then my response to you would be, "Then why did you date an idiot?"

Dating God's way should no doubt increase your prayer life. You will find yourself talking to God a lot about the person you are dating and looking for answers. With all the couples we've counseled with over the years, we have heard it all.

Here is a list of some of the most memorable statements we've heard from those who were seeking an answer from God:

1. God, if this is the right one for me, then let them wear a blue shirt to church today.
2. God, if I'm supposed to be with them, then let my mom call me out of nowhere and say, "I just made a cherry pie."
3. God, if this is the wrong person for me then let my dog speak to me and tell me. (That's usually when they don't want to chance God telling them it's the wrong person for them.)

No matter who you are in relationship with, you'll want to know whether or not this is a good person for you. There are different stages of relationships, as well, depending upon your age, where you are in life, and your desires.

In the beginning of a dating relationship, you're fine just knowing that you are not with a serial killer or a stalker. When the relationship progresses, you will want to know more. But you may never be one hundred percent sure of anything. That's the thing about relationships—there is no guarantee when it comes to dating.

You don't want to spend years of your life investing into the wrong person. On the other hand, if you two are right for each other, then you will be able to set some next steps for your relationship.

When Heather and I started dating, we knew there was no guarantee. We were both on a journey to discover if this was the right person for us. We had both been in previous relationships with people who were not right for us. We didn't want to waste any emotional time or energy if we saw signs that we were not a good potential match for one another.

She wasn't star stricken or influenced by the fact that I was the associate pastor of a large church. She wasn't convinced by my charisma, leadership, or ability to communicate an eloquent message from the stage to crowds of people.

I, on the other hand, had a different perspective. Being a single, available pastor, it's sort of the norm to hear people say, "I'm praying and believing that God will bring you a preaching woman," (aka Christian lingo for First Lady of the house). Well, Heather was not a preaching woman or a First Lady of the house, but I was drawn to her. With me being in ministry, I wanted to know deep down inside that neither one of us was a making a mistake in seeking a possible relationship or future marriage with each other. Whereas I had been in ministry for over fifteen years, Heather had never been in ministry a day in her life and had recently committed her life back to God a few years prior to us meeting each other. However, being a man, I was excited about this cute little blonde but didn't let her physical appearance convince me that she was "The One" for me.

As a result, we spent a lot of our dating time talking and asking questions. This turned out to be a good thing because it didn't allow us to spend lots of time in the "lovey dovey" stage, sitting all day and staring into each other's eyes, clueless to reality. As we discussed earlier in the book, we went out on dates with couples in leadership roles at our church.

As time went on, we started going out alone, just the two of us. These dates were still very intentional and we mostly went to places where we could sit and talk for hours and ask and answer many questions. We honestly found out so much about one another on our dates that it helped us navigate through conflict and disagreements.

I remember several times when we hit some pretty intense moments in which we didn't know if we were the right ones for each other. It probably happened about four times in our relationship; where one of us would see what we thought could be a possible deal-breaker. We didn't quit or say, "I'm done with this"; we would simply grab hands and say one of the most unselfish prayers you can pray in a dating relationship—God help us to resolve our differences or help us to walk away.

It is so important to remember that, while you are dating someone, God has not empowered you to change that person. That is not your job. If you build your relationship on you having to change, manipulate, and control someone, then you will be setting that relationship up for failure. Be honest and upfront, but not controlling.

In a relationship, two lives are involved and two futures are at stake. Many times, a person has a fear of losing someone, they try to adapt and change in a way that makes the other person happy. That is not good either. The person you are dating must see and experience the real you and not the false image that you think they want to see. Be yourself, ultimately trust God with your relationship, and be content with the outcome either way.

Don't Put the Cart before the Horse

I (Heather) know when you enter into a relationship, at some point you think this could be "The One." If you don't think that after spending a good amount of time together, maybe you shouldn't be dating that person.

Yes, you do have to be honest about your intentions if your intentions are to find a spouse. But you shouldn't tell them you think they're "The One" on the first date.

Sometimes women have the tendency to put the cart before the horse and start planning their dream wedding when they believe they've met their dream guy. I've even known a few women to buy their wedding dresses before they've even been engaged.

There are several reasons why that is a bad idea. First of all, the focus is not on the relationship as it should be; it's on the wedding. The wedding is only one day and the marriage is a lifetime. I can pretty much guarantee that you won't care that you had a Vera Wang dress on your wedding day when your marriage is crumbling because you didn't really know the person you married.

Second, if you didn't scare him off and he was thinking about moving forward and proposing, you have pretty much told him that you aren't waiting on his timing and you are going to do your own thing. This is not a good way to start a marriage.

Third, if he doesn't propose, you are stuck with a dress that you will never wear. When you meet someone else and get engaged, do you really want to wear the dress you picked out for your wedding to what's-his-name?

Guys, bear with me here as I talk a little bit about the wedding day. I realize this is a dating book, but, after all, you will eventually date someone that you will marry. Hopefully this will give you a little insight into the female mind.

When we are little girls, we dream of our wedding day—a perfect day with a beautiful dress, beautiful flowers, and a beautiful cake, surrounded by people we love. Some of the first images we see are of princesses getting saved by their prince. We put all this time and effort into this one day, but we don't always put all this effort into our future marriage. Yes, it's the day we dreamed of forever, but it's one day! Marriage is the rest of our lives. Shouldn't we put more effort into planning for the rest of our lives than we do into planning for one day?

A friend of mine told me she purchased her wedding dress, but she wasn't engaged yet. I asked her if they had been to premarital counseling and I never will forget her response. She said, "Don't you think it's too early to do premarital counseling?" I responded, "If it's not too early to buy a dress and plan for your wedding, then it's not too early to start premarital counseling."

Why is it okay to invest in the wedding, but not the marriage? You should be putting at least as much time into your premarital counseling as you should into planning for the big day. You should start premarital counseling before you even start looking for the dress or planning the wedding, because if you find out in premarital counseling that you're not for each other, then you have just saved yourself a bunch of time and money.

Women, we need to take our focus off of our wedding day and put it on the marriage. What good is a wedding going to be if you end up in a horrible marriage? When the priority is planning the wedding, what happens after the wedding day? What are your expectations for marriage?

We have a vision of what our wedding day looks like, but do we have a vision of what our marriage looks like? And is that vision realistic? Who's going to take out the garbage? Who's going to do the dishes and the cooking? Simple things add up. We all have different backgrounds and different customs or things we have done growing up. Are you compatible in those areas? If not, who is going to compromise?

So How Will I Know?

Let me be quite honest—if you're looking to be one hundred percent sure, then you will never know. Heather and I approached it this way: We wanted to make sure that there were certain things we could evaluate in our relationship that we both agreed were important enough to keep us moving forward.

Here are a few of those things:

1. Agreement

Amos 3:3 tells us, "How can two walk together unless they are in agreement?" Heather and I only kept moving forward as long as we were in agreement in our relationship. Now, don't get me wrong, you will never agree with anyone all the time. However, there were things that were important to each of us and values we wanted both of us to be in unity on.

2. Internal peace

This is a great indicator for forward movement. What I mean by this is that if you feel peace in your mind, spirit, and heart, then keep moving. When peace is interrupted, stop, investigate, and pinpoint what has disturbed the peace in the relationship. Once you've identified the disturbance, you can work together to bring resolve and restore the peace.

3. Our differences

It was very important for us to maintain our individuality and not try to change one another. Even though we both knew there were things about each of us that would have to change in order for this relationship to work, we never tried to change one another. We would always talk things through and pray about whatever it was. After that, we put it in God's hands.

When is it too soon to say I love you?

It's too soon on the first date! Or the second, or the third! It's too soon if you haven't had enough time to get to know them. If you don't know someone, how do you know you love them?

When do you meet the family?

This is going to depend on you and your family dynamics. To some people, this is of high value and something to be saved until later. To others, it's a very normal thing to do. First, make sure you both agree. Never force someone to meet your family when they aren't ready. Second, make sure you are both feeling the same way about each other. The main thing is to talk about the importance of this and to decide together.

When do you start talking about future plans?

Again, it's too soon on the first date. It's too soon if you haven't had enough time to get to know them. If you start talking about future plans with someone who isn't there yet, then you are going to completely scare them off.

If you go out on a date with someone and they make it clear that they are just dating to date and don't see marriage in their future, you already know their future plans are a few fun dates and probably not much more.

If marriage comes up in conversation on the first few dates, don't be afraid to tell the truth. Just because you are looking to get married doesn't mean that they are the one you want to marry. You are out on a date with them to try to find out.

What if "The One" Doesn't Work Out?

If "The One" doesn't work out, don't worry; there is always another one. Chances are, you have dated someone and you thought they were "The One," only to have that relationship end in a horrible breakup.

I (Adonis) remember dating someone I thought for sure was "The One" for me. I took her home to meet my family and everything. That was a huge step for me. I thought, "Wow! God is so awesome. Everything is falling into place and I'm finally going to be happy." Then, for reasons out of my control, she felt as if she would be making a mistake if she proceeded with the relationship.

I was devastated. It was so unfair. Things were going great—at least I thought so—and now this!

I spent weeks trying to convince her that I was the right person for her and that everything would work out. It was emotionally exhausting trying to convince her to change her mind day after day. As I look back on it now, I see that I was trying to force something to happen that just wasn't meant to be.

I had to reach a place where I could let go and move on. I had put all my hope and trust into one person and not God. I realized that God was bigger than one person and that I could still believe and trust Him to bring that special person into my life. And He did.

If you've found yourself in this situation, there is hope for you. There is a reason that it didn't work out. You can't see it now but one day you will be able to look back and see that God worked everything out for your good. Yes, it may hurt now, but it won't hurt forever. Continue to trust God and let time heal your broken heart. This too shall pass.

NAVIGATING CONFLICT

Every relationship experiences conflict every once in a while. Conflict does not mean that the relationship is doomed or headed in the wrong direction. It simply means that you both are human and as you continue to grow closer together you will find yourself facing conflict sooner or later. However, your ability to navigate through conflict will determine the success or failure of the relationship.

One of the first things we did when we started dating was take a personality profile test. We were in our mid-to-late thirties and our dating was very intentional as we were both looking toward a future marriage with whomever we were dating. We wanted all the help we could get so we met with one of our church leaders, Marci, who was a certified instructor for the personality profile assessment. She instructed us to take the test separately and not together. Heather and I didn't discuss the test or results until we had our follow up meeting with Marci. She took the time to explain the results and showed us areas where we would do well and areas that could be potential challenges.

We learned that we couldn't look at challenges or potential challenges as indicators that we shouldn't move forward with the relationship. Instead, Marci showed us how to successfully navigate through the challenges based on our individual personalities. For example, Heather and I had to learn to consider each other's personality to decide how to package and say what we were trying to communicate.

Heather learned that my personality doesn't handle spontaneous decisions very well. She couldn't just say that she wanted us to go do something right now without giving me time to process and plan.

I, on the other hand, learned that I couldn't just think that I'm the man and she should do whatever I tell her to do. I learned very quickly that her personality sees that as me trying to control her or force her to do something. This knowledge has definitely been a relationship saver for us and we still reflect back on the results of the test after five years of marriage as it continues to help us navigate through occasional conflict and disagreements. We recommend it to any dating couple that wants a better chance of walking through conflict at a more successful rate.

Occasional conflict is good; constant conflict is an indicator. One of my personal beliefs is that every dating couple needs to experience at least one good fight or big disagreement to see how the other person is going to act and respond throughout the conflict. It also gives you a chance to see how the both of you are able to bring about a peaceful resolution. You can tell a lot about a person when conflict hits in the relationship. You need to take notice of how you respond in conflict as well. Are you mad when you don't get your way? Do you find yourself getting aggravated very easily at the person you are dating? Are you mad at each other all the time? Do you fight over little things?

One thing is certain: There is no perfect dating relationship or marriage. All relationships have challenges. If someone ever tells you that they never have arguments in their relationship, they are lying to you.

Occasional Conflict

Don't be discouraged by occasional conflict. Conflict every now and then is not fatal and can prove to be very beneficial for the relationship and a future marriage. It's good to see how the two of you are able to handle and navigate through your disagreement or hurts. Conflict will even help you understand each other better.

Constant Conflict

Constant conflict is when you two are constantly fighting all the time. You're always irritated at one another. Things in your current relationship bring a constant irritation to you and may even prove to be detrimental to a future marriage if you proceed. Maybe you both are strong-willed and determined to have your way. Regardless, it's in these moments that you must sit down and evaluate. Ask these specific questions.

1. Have I sought out help from my accountability partner?
2. Am I trying to force something that wasn't meant to be?
3. Am I dating the wrong person?
4. Am I crazy? Are they crazy? (Trust me, some people are and just don't know it.)

Several years ago, I met with a young dating couple and it was very apparent to me within thirty minutes that they were probably very wrong for each other. Now, as a pastor, their expectation is more than likely for me to be just as excited as they are about a future marriage.

Over the years, I've made a decision that I would rather have the couple mad at me for sharing my unfavorable opinion than having them mad at me later for not making them aware of my concerns. If I see something that can and will have the potential to destroy a future marriage, I quickly and clearly bring this to their attention. Some people have on emotional blinders and can't see the reality of the situation when they are head-over-heels in love.

This young couple was headed to divorce court before they even got married. There was so much conflict going on in their relationship that they didn't need a pastor; they needed a referee. They were clearly not on the same page. In fact, they were not even in the same book. I couldn't believe my ears when, after spending two hours of telling me about all the fighting that they do, why they have fights, and whose fault the fights are, they both looked at me in full agreement and said, "But we know that God has brought us together for a reason and we are meant for each other. When we are married it won't be like this."

My first thought was to respond by calling bull. But as a pastor that wouldn't be too polite. I thought for a second longer and said, "So, you're telling me that out of all the billions of people on the planet, the best that God could do was bring two people together who fought constantly and irritated the heck out of each other all the time?"

Long story short, they got mad at me and walked away never

to seek my advice or counsel again. They went to the justice of the peace and got married, and then had to go to divorce court a few months later.

I said all that to say this: If there is constant conflict without any signs of resolve, then you might be dating the wrong person. It might be time to let go and move on. Marriage doesn't change anything; it only enhances what's already there.

Healthy Conflict

Healthy conflict is when a disagreement, argument, or fight leads to a growing moment and better understanding of each other. Healthy conflict always ends in peace.

It's important to examine the reason of the conflict first. This is a great time to be honest and very open in your communication instead of staying silent and keeping everything bottled up inside. When you're hurt by the person you are dating, you must understand that this will bring conflict if you don't communicate it to them. What usually happens is that the hurt person has a tendency to not share the hurt with the person who caused it.

No matter how little or big the situation was that hurt you, it needs to be communicated. Maybe they don't even know that they said something or did something that hurt you. They could be clueless to the fact that you are upset at them for something that they did or said three weeks ago. This is not good for the relationship.

Ladies, this is not the time to keep it from him and talk to your girlfriends about it.

Guys, this is not the time to hold it in until the big blow up moment that could really cause damage.

When Heather and I were dating, it was very hard for me to

let her know when she said or did something that hurt me. My pride would keep me from communicating to her that I was hurt because I saw that as a sign of weakness. I thought I would be less of a man if I told her she hurt me.

One time we were having a conversation on a certain subject that eventually turned into a disagreement. Now keep in mind, it is perfectly normal to have disagreements. Anyway, she said something that unintentionally hurt me. My pride kept me from communicating to her in that moment that I was hurt. I wanted to be strong in front of her. No way was I going to let a woman know that she hurt me!

This only caused me to replay that hurt over and over in mind for days until it eventually affected my time with her. I was instantly irritated by things she said and did from that moment on, because it was all being filtered through the hurt that I was constantly rehearsing in my mind.

Several days passed and she had no idea that she hurt me. Finally noticing my indifferent behavior, she asked me what was wrong. At first, I kept saying that nothing was wrong and that I was fine. Then I realized that I needed to communicate my hurt so that we could discuss, resolve, and move forward. When I finally communicated what I felt, we were able to rehash what had happened. She explained that she didn't mean it that way and she had no idea that it hurt me. I then realized that I took it the wrong way and should have spoken up sooner. It's the old saying of "making a mountain out of a mole hill."

From that moment on, we've learned to speak up as soon as an offense takes place. If one of us gets hurt or offended by what the other one says, we immediately let them know. This gives

A Note on Being Hurt

When I reference being hurt by the person you are in a relationship with, I am not talking about being hurt by physical or verbal abuse. If that is happening to you, then it is in your best interest to end this relationship. If you feel trapped by fear, then please talk to a family member, a pastor, or a close friend so that you can receive counsel and direction on how to get to a place of safety. If you're reading this and you're thinking that you can't leave that person because you love them and they love you, and you're hoping that the abuse will stop, then maybe it's a soul tie that is keeping you in that abusive relationship. That is not love you are feeling, and the soul tie needs to be broken so that you can move forward with your life.

the other person a chance to explain their comment and apologize. We've come to find out that often times the hurt is unintentional and usually is just something that was taken the wrong way.

We strive to keep open communication. We also know that we both love each other and would never do anything intentional to cause hurt or offense in the other so we listen and hear each other out without being defensive.

The moment you start being defensive, it gives an opportunity for one of you to start feeling attacked. Being successful at healthy conflict takes work on both parts and a common belief that you both want to keep and guard the peace in your relationship.

Signs of Unhealthy Conflict

1. Holding a Grudge: This is a good indicator that you are still holding something against the other person. It's also an indicator that there has been no resolve.

2. Manipulation: You are now manipulating the other person because of something they did. You are no longer trusting but now controlling their every action by taking advantage of their mistake.

3. Avoidance: The more space you put between each other during conflict, the harder it is to reach a place of resolve.

4. Verbal Abuse: Guys, listen up. Women are not wired like us. We tend to be masculine even in our tone of voice. Yelling or raising your voice at her will do more damage than good. If she is afraid of you, that is definitely unhealthy.

Discussing your Relational Conflict with Others

We looked at this earlier in the book, but it's worth going over again. Discussing conflict with your best friend or a family member may prove to be harmful to your relationship. I am not saying that you shouldn't confide in a best friend or family member when going through conflict with the person you are dating; there are many parents and friends who can offer great advice and support. I would, instead, say that it's better to be cautious on the details of what you share. You are not hiding the relationship; you are protecting the relationship. You are not perfect and neither is the person you are dating.

Let's say you are going through a pretty rough time in your relationship because of something that the other person did. It was totally their fault and now you are feeling hurt. You then reach out to a family member or a best friend and share the details of what they did. That family member or best friend is likely to feel your hurt or disappointment from an emotional standpoint because of their connection with you.

Now, the huge problem with this is that you are still in the middle of navigating this particular conflict and hurt. Time goes on and you and the person you are dating reach a place of forgiveness, resolution, and healing. That is all glorious until you find out that your family member or best friend is now holding a grudge against the person you are dating. Like I said before, all of a sudden, Thanksgiving Dinner at your house is very awkward.

The bottom line is that you may forgive but your family or friends may not. I'm not saying this always happens but it is something to think about when discussing your relational conflict with others.

IS ONLINE DATING
FOR CHRISTIANS?

Online dating has come to be a reality of everyday life in the singles arena. With dating sites, Facebook, Twitter, live chat, texting, and much more, the ability to connect with others is ever present and within reach. Let's face it, if you have a cell phone, the ability and accessibility to date and build a relationship is literally at your fingertips. Recent statistics say that there are fifty-four million singles in the United States and, of the fifty-four million, forty million have tried online dating.

I (Adonis) have met many happily married Christian couples that met online and had a wonderful dating experience. The reality of this is that online dating is a tool in which many couples, Christian and Non-Christian, are finding their true love and happily ever after.

This is one of those areas in which I believe there is no right or wrong answer, only opinions. There are always pros and cons to any online dating site. I would suggest that if you are wanting to date God's way then you might want to start with Christian dating sites. This narrows the field but it doesn't guarantee that everyone on that site is a Christian, or that you will share the same beliefs. In the end, you still have to trust God, use wisdom, and stick to the standards and guidelines you have set.

Here's the story of some friends of ours who met online:

Luis and Dianne

On May 16, 1997, I was sitting in front of my computer just watching the messages scroll up in an AOL chat room, when I got an instant message (IM) from someone with the screen name, Luis1959, just like in the movie *You've Got Mail*. It said, "So, Dianne, I see you are a Christian."

I'd heard about stalkers on the Internet, but I didn't really put much stock in it until that moment when someone I'd never met sent me an IM calling me by my first name and somehow knew that I was a Christian.

My stomach began fluttering and as quickly as I could type, I sent a return IM: "Who is this? How do you know my name, and how do you know I'm a Christian?"

Almost as quickly, I got a reply IM: "I read your profile and guessed at your name."

I felt like a complete idiot to say the least, as my own screen name was Dianne1954 and my profile included my favorite quote ". . . this one thing I do, forgetting those things which are behind, and reaching forth unto those things which are before, I press toward the mark for the prize of the high calling of God in Christ Jesus" (Philippians 3:13–14).

Several IMs followed between us, and Luis ended up sending me his phone number. We spent thirty minutes on the phone that day and never missed a day talking since then.

I lived in Nashville, Tennessee, and he was in Binghamton, New York. After talking with Luis every day for almost a month and IMing back and forth, we decided it was time to meet, so he flew down to meet me on June 13. We spent the weekend getting to know each other a little more, and he went to church with my children and me before catching his flight back to New York on Sunday afternoon.

Over the next few months and years, there were flights and long drives made by each of us, even bringing our families together in Charlotte, North Carolina, to meet each other at a baseball game.

Finally, in July of 1998, Luis made the decision to move to Nashville. We continued getting to know each other over the next year, and in July of 1999, he asked me to marry him and, of course, I said yes! We were married on January 1, 2000, in Franklin, Tennessee. We both feel we have been blessed with a gift from God in each other.

Meeting someone online doesn't make them a predator, nor does meeting someone at church make them a Christian. I do believe there are pros and cons to *any* form of dating and you have to be wise and be cautious regardless. Yes, you might be taking a risk meeting someone online, but the same goes for whomever you meet or wherever you meet them.

Any person you meet for the first time is a stranger until you get to know them. I would suggest that if you try online dating, it would be wise for you to set a date in which you can meet the person face to face after you've talked online or on the phone for a while and feel pretty comfortable meeting them. Even then, I would suggest meeting them in a public place. We've all seen the news or television reality shows in which a person thinks they are dating a specific person online and it turns out to be someone totally opposite of the pictures they have seen.

Involve your accountability partner in this as well. Make no mistake about it, the longer you have an online dating experience, the more your emotions are attached. You don't have to be physical or even sexually involved in order for there to be intimacy in the relationship. Once again, your accountability partner is able to view this from a different perspective with no emotional attachment.

Should You Date More Than One Person?

Dating more than one person is not a good idea; it's a reality TV show. Reality shows try to convince us that dating multiple people over a course of three months can lead to meeting your soul mate and living happily ever after. What man or woman in their right mind is going to stand in line waiting to be picked by a person who has dated, kissed, or had sex with almost all of them?

It's okay to talk to several people, initially, to decide if you like them, and to see if there are mutual interests and commonalities. But once two people have decided they like each other and would like to date, it's not a good idea to date more than one person.

When someone dates more than one person, they are either hiding the relationships or the people they are in the relationship with are dating other people as well, which is usually called an open dating relationship. This still usually causes someone to eventually end up hurt in the long run.

Online Dating: Love It or Hate It

Singles are either completely for it or completely against it. I know people that have had bad experience with it and others who have met their spouses online. One of my wise friends told me this, "Why do we find it so crazy to meet someone online that is selected as a potential match based on our personality and likes, but don't find it crazy to meet someone at a bar that we know nothing about?" Granted, you may not be looking for someone in a bar, but you may be looking for someone at church that you know nothing about. At church, at least you are hoping they are Christian, but unfortunately that's not always true.

If you've explored all other options, then why not give it a try?

Here are some tips to help you have a positive experience instead of a negative one:

- Be honest when filling out your profile. Don't portray someone you aren't.
- Post a recent picture of yourself. You wouldn't want someone posting a ten-year-old picture of themselves only to find out they look nothing like their picture.
- Filling out your profile is the perfect opportunity to be upfront with what you are and aren't looking for. Be clear about it. If you put the importance of your faith out there, then they already know where you stand.
- When you sign up and you say you are willing to meet singles in any part of the country, you better be willing to move to any part of the country.
- Don't spend months getting to know someone before you actually meet them in person. If you've been talking for a month, it may be a good time to meet.

171

- Do your homework and run an online search on them to make sure they are who they say they are. This is a huge tool right at your fingertips. Try searching for yourself and click on images and see what comes up. You may be surprised!
- Don't share information you wouldn't share with someone in person.
- When you do meet in person, make sure it is in a safe place like a restaurant, coffee shop, etc. and either have someone nearby or at the very least someone who knows where you are.
- Don't let someone talk to you inappropriately online and expect something different from them in person.
- Don't get discouraged by suitors you aren't interested in contacting you. After all, you're on an online dating site, this is bound to happen.
- On the flip side, don't get discouraged if you aren't getting contacted. There is someone out there for everyone. You may want to have a friend or spiritual authority take a look at your profile and make sure you are portraying yourself in an honest, yet best way possible.
- If something seems fishy, it probably is!

Don't use the line that online dating is dangerous as an excuse to not do it. When you do it, just be smart about it. When I (Heather) am not a wife, mother, cook, baker, golfer, counselor, teacher, or author, I'm a Forensic Scientist and do Forensic DNA. Yes, just like on the CSI shows, but trust me when I say it's not that glamorous.

Crimes typically do not happen in big fancy houses like you see on television shows. I tell you this because I want to stress the importance, for women especially, not to put yourselves in dangerous or potentially dangerous situations when it comes to dating. If you go on a date with someone you've met online, have a friend nearby on a stakeout. The worst that can happen (at least if it goes well) is you fall in love, get married, and have a funny story to look back and laugh at! If it doesn't work out, at least you tried . . . and you probably have a story now to share with your friends.

Same goes for the guys. In this day and age, you can never be too careful.

We counseled with a woman who was attractive, intelligent, and put-together, yet hadn't gone out on a date in twelve years. After talking with her, we figured out she hadn't been on a date because she wasn't putting herself out there and was turning down dates because she was looking for the perfect person.

I hate to burst everyone's bubble, but there is no one perfect person!

Let's say she finally went on a date. How do you think she would do? Probably not too well because she has no experience dating! I'm not saying date every single person who asks you, but don't go twelve years without dating either.

Don't lose out on someone who may have been good for you because you are rusty or out of practice. Even if that means going out with someone who invited you out that you don't think you are interested in, get the experience and be open. You never know when you may or may not click with someone. You may not be super attracted to them, but once you get to know them you may find out you have a lot in common and, suddenly, they start to become more and more attractive.

Stay dedicated and determined. It's not always easy to put yourself out there and there will be times that you will face rejection. Don't give up on yourself. Make it a point to learn from your mistakes so you don't make the same ones over again.

FACEBOOK OFFICIAL:

Sharing Your Relationship with the World via Social Media

I t's always exciting when you enter into a relationship. One of the first tendencies you have is to share your good news with the world by updating your relationship status on your profile. With a few clicks, you instantly go from being single to in a relationship and everyone knows it.

The only problem with that is you tend to only share all the great things about your relationship. You constantly post things like, "I've got the best boyfriend in the world," with a photo of a dozen roses on your desk at work. Or you share things like, "My girlfriend is the best," with a photo of the chocolate, caramel covered brownies that she surprised you with.

Now, don't get me wrong, that's all fine and dandy, but don't get trapped trying to uphold an image in front of people. When the relationship starts having conflicts and struggles, you tend to lose sight of reality because you have been portraying an image of success and pure delight to the entire world. When there's trouble in your relationship, you now find it hard to reach out for help. You become bombarded with thoughts that everyone will think you have been lying all this time about your fabulous relationship and you certainly don't want to look like a liar. The real damage gets done when you masquerade the trouble in hopes that the problem will fix itself so no one will ever know, and you can make another social media post about your wonderful relationship via social media.

If this is happening in your relationship, then you need to understand that your relationship is held captive by the social media appearance you created. Only by being honest and truthful with your accountability partner or someone you trust will allow your relationship to get the help that it needs. Don't get caught in the trap of ignoring the reality in order to keep the favorable opinions of others via the Internet.

During our dating process, we were very intentional about not posting or sharing anything via social media. I (Adonis) am not saying that this way is the way for everybody, nor am I saying that posting about your relationship via social media will destroy it. There are many dating couples that post about their relationships and everything continues to go fine. I think you both should have a say so in whether or not you feel comfortable blasting your love life out there to the entire world.

Status: In a Relationship

Some people are private while others are social media butter-flies. For us, we both experienced a freedom in our relationship without the whole world offering their advice, input, approval, disapproval, or congratulations. This allowed us to get to know each other without any expectations from others. We didn't have to live up to anything that was posted on the Internet.

Basically, we had time without any interference to figure out if we were the right ones for each other. We even knew that if the relationship didn't work out then it would be a little easier for us to move on without having to explain to the whole world what happened and why we felt like this relationship couldn't work. We had many mutual friends between us and we knew that it could be potentially awkward for them as well. We would much rather have people share in the joy of our marriage than to have them share in the joy of the early stages of a relationship that had the potential of not working out.

How many times have you seen a couple go through a breakup and all those cute romantic posts turn ugly, mean, and vengeful? Someone always wants to be the victim and tries to get everyone to sympathize with them. Bashing someone on social media only makes you look bad. If you are ever in this situation, then make the mature decision to not lash out via the Internet. You will be thankful in time that you didn't.

Looking back now, we know that it was the right thing for us to do and we are so glad we did it that way. We never posted anything via social media until we announced our engagement. We were very intentional about keeping our relationship out of the public eye as much as possible. We weren't hiding our relationship; we were protecting our relationship. By then, we were already 100 percent committed to each other and a future marriage.

Status: In a Relationship and It's Complicated

Yes, you better believe it. People actually add this remark to their relationship status. You've just told the whole world and all your friends and family members that you are in a messed up relationship. You and I both know that just because it's complicated doesn't mean that something bad is going on. However, that's not the way it's perceived on social media.

You've just invited unwanted opinions to flood your inbox and you can only imagine what your friends and family are thinking about the person you are dating. If you are in a complicated relationship, you certainly don't need the opinions of the world flooding your mind and influencing your actions.

Here are a few questions to think about if you are in a complicated relationship. Ask yourself these questions and respond with a truthful answer. Once you know the truth, it will bring about a freedom in you and empower you to be free from a complicated relationship, whether that's being free by letting go and moving on, or being free by eliminating the factors that bring about the complication in your relationship.

> "And you shall know the truth, and the truth shall
> make you free." (John 8:32 NKJV)

1. Why am I in this relationship?

Obviously, there must be a good reason for anyone to be in a complicated relationship. Unfortunately, very few are able to find a solution and stay trapped in a relationship that continues to bring a level of frustration and non-satisfaction.

2. Am I making an unhealthy compromise because I am afraid of losing them?

If there's one thing that can add a high level of complication to any relationship, it is premarital sex. This certainly brings an emotional roller coaster ride on your journey filled with unmet expectations.

3. Is this complication a potential deal-breaker?

If it's bringing a high level of frustration now, then it will bring a higher level of frustration later.

4. Am I the one who's making this complicated?

In every relationship, there is always taking and giving. Some have to make more compromises than others depending on the dynamics and factors in the relationship. If you're in a relationship that requires you to readjust your expectations, then you must decide if you are okay with that.

It would be unfair for the other person if your expectations were unrealistic in sight of the reality of the relationship. But it may also be unfair to you to have to change so much to fit this relationship.

DO DATING
AND TEXTING MIX?

Just like anything else, texting and dating comes with its own list of pros and cons. It is definitely a technology tool that, if used properly, can help you along in your dating process. There's nothing like receiving a text during the day from your special someone that lets you know that they're thinking about you. Texting is also a great tool for those who are a little timid for those first face-to-face encounters.

There are a lot of guys who are in the same boat I was. They are shy, intimidated, or just plain too nervous to start out with a simple conversation. Some guys are afraid of rejection and it's much easier to be rejected via text than it is face-to-face.

When I first started noticing Heather, it was difficult for me to communicate to her. I felt very awkward for several reasons. The main reason was the fact that I was a pastor of her church.

Another reason was that my personality tends to be a little introverted and reserved at times. It's just not in my nature to approach a girl and start up a conversation.

Texting became a great resource and tool for me during the early stages of our pre-dating days. When I led the golfing life group at the church, text and email were a formal way of communicating to those in the group. When I found out that Heather played golf, it was a no brainer for me to try and get her to sign up.

I remember the day I approached her by saying, "Hey I know you are new here and I know you like to play golf. How about signing up for my golf life group? All you have to do is give me your phone number and email address so I can include you in the communications distribution list." Once I got her contact information I began to email her along with the rest of the group. Those emails eventually turned into me following up with her via text to make sure she got the email that I sent to the group. Shortly, those text messages went from being golf related to me just asking her how she was doing. It didn't take to long for her to figure out that I was interested in her.

My text messages to her were never inappropriate, nor did they ever cross any lines. I kept it very clean, short, and conservative. I was not hiding behind the text trying to be someone I wasn't. If you are going to use texting as a resource and tool, you need to have some guidelines of what not to do.

Avoiding Texting Mistakes

1. Don't argue via text.

Even a simple text can leave room for assumptions. When you text something, the other person can't see your facial expression and it leaves too much room for interpretation. You take a huge risk of the situation going from bad to worse. It's best to reserve your arguing for a face-to-face conversation.

If the other person is persistent and trying to get you to settle an issue via text then do your relationship a favor and respond as nicely as you can and as short as you can, and let them know that you are looking forward to settling this issue with them in person.

2. No sexting or inappropriate text messages.

This only stimulates and increases your desire for each other more. Furthermore, it's just a horrible idea to take a picture of yourself naked, or even half naked, and hit send on your phone. We've all heard the story where a couple breaks up and then an angry boyfriend forwards a picture to friends of his ex. It's called Cyber Revenge and it's not good. Ask yourself, "Would I be comfortable showing my text trail to my accountability partner?"

Ladies, trust me. Speaking from a guy's perspective, we know how to "fish." It's very easy to tell when a guy crosses the line in his communication. I've seen this time and time again—a guy sends a text message trying to fish and see if the woman bites. The woman responds in a joking manner, trying to be nice. The guys sees that as a nibble on the bait and keeps on fishing. Soon afterwards, that text message has led to a full-blown phone sex encounter. It isn't long until the physical sexual encounters take place because they have already crossed that line of passionate, lustful sexting via text messages.

The moment the first inappropriate message happens, you need to recognize it and not respond politely. If you bite the bait, then sooner or later you will be hooked. A lot of women make the mistake of nicely responding via text to an inappropriate text because they don't want to hurt the guy. It's better to hurt him now than to have him hurt you later.

Remember, the best thing to do is stop it as soon as you see it. If they start sexting, you start "nexting" and move on to the next one.

3. No serial texting.

Be careful not to overload the person you are dating with a million text messages every day. You're becoming an irritation more than a person they love spending time with. In the beginning, it may be fun and enjoyable, but it gets real old real quick and can easily be mistaken for insecurity or control. The person may see you as someone who needs to know where they are and what they are doing every second of their day.

Don't just take for granted that the person you are dating likes to have their phone blown up by all your little gestures of love throughout their day. This is definitely a conversation you should have and see what the other person thinks. The last thing you want to do is run someone off by being too intrusive.

"CAN'T YOU JUST BE HAPPY FOR ME?"

When Others Are Not Excited about Your Relationship

We all want everyone to be just as excited about our relationship as we are. The harsh reality is that you will never have everyone on board with you. Your friends or family members may be the ones to shock you the most. But you shouldn't need everyone on board with you.

A dating relationship involves two people. If there's a third party involved, then we would be talking about a love triangle and we've all seen how those end up as an episode on *Dateline*. There is a time and place for third-party influence and that should fall under the guidelines of your accountability partner. You should always have an open door for that person to speak candidly to you about the relationship.

Tim and Amy Coleman

We received mixed responses from our families when we started dating. Tim's parents were accepting and our siblings, for the most part, were open to the idea. Unfortunately, my father wasn't thrilled about our dating and he was completely opposed to our engagement. During those years, Tim responded to hurtful comments and gestures with complete love for my dad.

After almost three years together, our wedding day arrived. Despite his reservations, my dad showed up in the middle of our rehearsal dinner and returned the next day to walk me down the aisle. There were a few stressful moments, but our wedding was beautiful with our pastor and Tim's dad officiating.

Three years after the wedding, we welcomed our first son, Camry. I still vividly remember handing our week-old baby to my dad. It was as if I had handed him ammunition against this battle he was fighting. Camry broke something in him.

A year and a half later, my dad had a brush with death after congestive heart failure. As he lay there in his hospital bed, he shared his journey with me. He said he never considered himself to be a bigot, listing several examples of his accepting outlook of other races. Our engagement announcement years earlier had seriously challenged how accepting he really was. Unlike my mother, who had a genuine concern with where we would live and raise our children, my dad simply didn't want the "blood lines" to cross.

As I stood in his hospital room, he tearfully told me of the beginning of his transformation the day I gave him his first grandson. He realized then that God brought a perfect baby from of our union.

We will celebrate twenty years of marriage this fall and my dad has been a huge part of our family—loving all of us completely.

However, I want to talk about family and friends on either side that may not share the same enthusiasm for the person you are dating. It's important for the two of you to be on the same page when it comes to this. This is also a time in which the relationship can and should be tested.

Interracial Relationships

Heather and I knew that, although we live in a much different world today than we did fifty years ago, interracial relationships are still frowned upon by some people. I had been away from my family for such a long time that I wasn't concerned what their opinion about Heather would be. On the other hand, I knew Heather was close to her family and I didn't know what their opinion would be of me dating their daughter.

We went out to dinner one night with Tim and Amy Coleman, an interracial couple that are leaders in our church. Tim is black and Amy is white. They have an amazing marriage and they love sharing their story with others.

They were telling us their dating story and how Amy's

5 Things to Never Say to a Woman

1. "I think you better skip the dessert." This implies something a woman never, ever wants to hear.

2. "Is it that time of the month?" Say this to a woman, and you are certain to get your head taken off.

3. "You need to just get over it." She's about to be getting over you!

4. "That dress looks nice on you, but . . ." Anything you say after that is irrelevant.

5. "Your friend is really hot." Do we really need to mention this one?

5 Things to Never Say to a Guy

1. "My biological clock is ticking" or "My eggs are getting old." Bad move, enough said.
2. "Are you sure you can afford that?"
3. "My last boyfriend used to bring me here all the time."
4. "Does this dress make me look fat?" This is a trap and you should never set it.
5. "You're my boyfriend, right?" If you have to ask then he probably isn't.

dad had a very hard time with her dating Tim. When they decided to get married, he had an even harder time with that. They were not even sure he was going to come to the wedding. Still, Tim and Amy made a commitment to each other and were not going to let the opinions of others influence them in a negative way.

They moved forward without the agreement of her Dad. Now, years later, all is good and Amy's dad is definitely a part of their lives.

In a relationship, there must be a high level of commitment that is not swayed by the opinions or disapproval of others. Your relationship may one day be tested by a family member or friend you love.

If you are dating someone and see the signs of them being manipulated or controlled by the opinions of others, then I strongly advise you to proceed with caution. To me, it's a deal-breaker, and if ignored can lead to a future life of misery in a potential marriage.

Years ago, I counseled with an interracial couple; he was white, and she was black. At first, things seemed to be going very well. Then, one day, I received a call from the guy and he stated that everything was going fine in their relationship, but that his parents didn't agree with him being in an interracial relationship. My first thought was, "You're a grown man and haven't lived with your parents for years and should be able to make your own decisions." I didn't say that but I sure wanted to.

As he continued to talk, it became very clear to me that his parents still had a strong influence in his life that directly affected his ability to function in this relationship. He began to question the relationship that was going well. He began to doubt and fear that maybe he was making a mistake. The girl, on the other hand, is one of the kindest, sweetest people you will ever meet. In fact, I would have to say that she was definitely a step up and in the right direction for him. Unfortunately for the guy, he gave his parents control of his life in this area instead of giving God control.

I think many times, as Christians, we misinterpret the Scripture about honoring our parents: "Honor your father and your mother, as the Lord your God has commanded you, so that you may live long and that it may go well with you" (Deuteronomy 5:16 NIV). This scripture instructs us to honor our parents. It doesn't say anything about allowing them to control our life's decision. It is very possible to honor them while setting some healthy boundaries for them as well.

In my opinion, it cost that guy a great relationship and a wonderful woman. On the other hand, it probably saved her from a life of misery and awkward, stressful holidays with the in-laws.

Heather and I weren't immune to this scrutiny either. When we announced our engagement, we were surprised that not everyone in our family shared our same joy and excitement. It hurt the both of us to think that a family member would have the opinion that we shouldn't be together because of our different races.

This was a big test in our relationship. It was important for both of us to see that the other person did not waiver in commitment simply because a family member disapproved of our relationship. We assured each other of our commitment and love for each other and made the decision that if this family member did not accept each of us, then they would have neither of us in their lives. We grabbed hands and prayed, and put this situation in God's hands.

Long story short, this family member had a completely different attitude within a week's time and now they are a big part of our family. Even better, Heather and I grew closer through the experience.

What if You Are Already Dating Someone?

If you are reading this book and are already dating, what do you do? It's not too late to go back and make sure you are following these things. If you aren't, make them right.

If you are a believer and your date isn't, then you need to make the decision whether or not you want to be with them. If you decide to remain together, then you need to realize that you may always be unequally yoked and walking in different directions and you now need to manage it.

Are you carrying baggage or are they? Always start with yourself; that is the one thing you can change. If you are carrying baggage, you need to give that baggage to God. If your date is carrying baggage, talk about it and the way it makes you feel.

As far as sexual purity, you can change your view after reading this or you may be in church one day where God speaks to your heart and says He doesn't want this for you anymore. God will honor what you do.

You can always say, from this point forward, we are going to be sexually pure. God will honor you if you make that decision. You just have to ask for forgiveness and then put your guardrails in place. If you are living together, don't fool yourself into thinking you have guardrails in place.

If you already have soul ties, take a step back and ask God for forgiveness and how to help you. Start to focus on getting to know one another again. If you engaged in sexual activity already in the relationship then it's time to stop, take the time to get to know each other better on a deeper emotional and spiritual level.

Think of it like fasting. You are denying yourself of pleasurable foods so you can focus on God. Do that in your relationship. Take away your physical relationship and focus on each other. Go to your spiritual authority, or find spiritual authority, and ask them to look at your relationship and point out areas that need guidance or fixing. If you don't have a spiritual authority, ask yourself if your relationship is honoring God or dishonoring God.

Overall, it's up to you to do a relationship assessment and figure out where you both are. The assessment will show where to go from there.

Waiting to Date

I know we've talked a lot about dating intentionally or dating to prepare for marriage. I also know that some of you reading this aren't ready to get married. If that's you, that doesn't mean that you shouldn't date.

Dating is a way of getting to know what you do and don't like in a relationship. Let's face it, we aren't all going to be perfect at dating and most won't get it right on the first try. That's great for you if you do, but if you don't, that's okay. As long as you do it God's way, without engaging in a sexual relationship, and do it with honesty and integrity, then it's going to be a learning experience. Hopefully one that you can take away lessons from and make improvements about yourself and upon your expectations.

It seems that the trend nowadays is to get married later in life. Most of that is due to further education and careers. I'm all for that, but don't be someone who doesn't date because you don't have time for it and then end up dateless once you are ready ten years later.

Take the story of Beth, she was very dedicated to her schoolwork and didn't date in high school or college. She had been asked out many times, but always turned her suitors down because she made up her mind she wasn't going to date in high school or college.

Beth was content and started the career she had always dreamed of. When Beth decided she was ready to get married, there were no longer any suitors. Why? It certainly was not because her looks or because her personality had changed, but because Beth was no longer around many singles. Most of her friends and coworkers were in relationships or married. Even the former singles in her church around her age were now married.

The reality was that Beth was now set in her routine and was no longer in an environment where she was going to meet anyone. If Beth wanted to find someone to date, that would require her to step out of her routine and maybe even out of her comfort zone to find other singles.

Unlike a college education or career, marriage isn't something you just set out and accomplish. It's something that takes two people and starts with dating.

STILL SINGLE, SEARCHING, AND SICK OF IT:

Winning Over Loneliness

Chances are that everyone has fought this battle at one time or another in their lives. It's an emotional rollercoaster with the ability to take you on a journey in your mind, heart, and desires.

In an attempt to bring comfort and encouragement to Christian singles, the church coined a phrase that said, "Be single and satisfied." The ironic part about that is the advice to be single and satisfied usually came from married people who had been married for years and had probably forgotten what is was like to be single. They came up with stuff like, "Fall in love with Jesus first and then love yourself." Once again, I think this was an attempt to give a super spiritual answer rather than address the core issue of a single person who loves Jesus and themselves but was overwhelmed with a sense of loneliness and not being satisfied.

Loneliness is not a bad word, nor does it mean you are less spiritual and a weak Christian. It simply means that you have a desire to find that soul mate and spend the rest of your life with the person of your dreams. It's like being content and discontent at the same time. You are passionate about God. You love yourself, but you still have a sense of being unfulfilled.

Don't beat yourself up for feeling this way. It doesn't mean that you are failing in your Christian walk; it means that you are human.

I can recall all my single years of battling the feelings of loneliness. I'm not going to lie; it was horrible. Wanting to find that special someone and spend the rest of my life with them seemed like a fading dream that would become less attainable year after year. The worst part was being around dating and married couples and seeing them so happy. When you're single, every married couple appears happy. They're not, so don't rush your dating process to get there.

Still, seeing other happy couples magnifies your feelings of loneliness and sends you off on a tangent of desperately trying to find what they have. The older I got, the worse the feeling became. Unfortunately, I didn't respond correctly to the feelings of loneliness in the beginning and, therefore, lost that battle several times. It drove me to enter relationships I had no business being involved in.

In my right mind, I would have never entered those relationships in the first place, but I was operating through the filters of my loneliness. I felt entitled to happiness. Others were happy and, by all means, I was going to be happy too.

I was so blinded to the fact that I was in a very vulnerable state in my life and I got involved in relationships without talking to God or others about it first. I ignored the advice of others who cared for me and saw that I was making poor choices and bad decisions. I saw their advice as something that was trying to take away my potential happiness. I went forward anyway and ended up going through situations that I never thought in a million years that I'd be in. Those relationships never brought me happiness and they actually ended up hurting me as well as others.

How to Battle Loneliness

1. Don't be led by your feelings.

When your emotions get out of control, it becomes very easy to take a downward spiral into a pit of despair. You must gain control of these emotions quickly or they will cause you to make choices that you will no doubt regret.

This feeling often times comes along with the emotion of fear. The older you get, the more you start thinking that you better hurry up and find that right person before you are too old and it's too late. This is where it's easy to get into the wrong relationship. Your pursuit of finding someone should never be driven by fear. Don't let the fear of never finding someone cause you to settle for the wrong one. Find strength and comfort in the Bible and begin to meditate on what God has to say about the situation.

In the Bible, God even tells us His thoughts on man being alone and His solution to this situation.

> "Then the Lord God said, 'It is not good for the man
> to be alone. I will make a helper who is just right for
> him.'" (Genesis 2:18 NLT)

There it is. God is fully aware of the desires we have to be with someone. In fact, He's the one who gives us those desires. Despite the Christian lingo of being single and satisfied, it was never His intention for us to independently make ourselves happy. God never looked at Adam and said, "Don't worry, Adam. I know you are alone but as long as you have Me you don't need anyone else." No, it says that God saw the man by himself and knew He needed to do something to deal with the man's loneliness. So, God made a woman.

You have to trust that God is preparing that special person for you.

2. Don't isolate yourself.

In other words, don't become a hermit. Many times, singles become unaware that they are actually doing this. It's easy to get frustrated if you haven't had any success in dating. You begin to feel like a third wheel while hanging out with your friends who are dating or married. The tendency is to eventually give up, sit at home, and wait for God to bring that person to your front door. Chances are that will never happen unless the FedEx

David and Phyllis

I (Adonis) love the story of my assistant David and his wife Phyllis. They are one of the sweetest couples you could ever meet.

David attended a local church and was a part of a singles class. Phyllis was invited by her sister to attend. At first, she was very reluctant but she ended up going anyway.

Had Phyllis not attended that class with her sister, she would have never met David. Phyllis continued to attend the singles class each week and they talked more and more until David finally asked Phyllis out. With over thirty years of marriage, they still act like newlyweds.

person knocks on your door and it's love at first sight. I'm not saying that can't happen but the chances are slim to none, with slim being out of town.

This is when you have to force yourself to stay active in your social life. Look for opportunities to serve at your church or in your community. Do whatever you need to do to stay around people.

If your church has a singles group that is active, then look into joining that. Now, I'm not talking about one of the singles groups that sit around all day talking about dating and finding the right person. I'm talking about a singles group that is all about building relationships, having community, and doing activities together. This will keep your mind in a healthy place and it may also serve as the very doorway that leads you to meeting that special someone.

Your motivation for joining a singles group shouldn't only be to meet that special person, but chances are you will never meet that special person while sitting at home alone.

3. Don't date for a quick fix.

Believe it or not, there are some people who simply date so that they won't be alone. They have an overwhelming need to have somebody, anybody, in their life. This is very unhealthy, as they end up going from person to person and one bad break up after another. In the long run, this does so much emotional and spiritual damage to a person. Jumping into another relationship is not the answer to healing a broken heart. God is.

On the other hand, some people jump into a relationship to get over the hurt or pain from the last one. This almost never works out well. They are hurting so badly that they feel like another person can numb the hurt or take the pain away all together. This is very unfair to the other person, as well.

Let's say you yourself have just gone through a bad breakup. Your partner cheated on you, and now you are an emotional wreck and don't know what to do. Instead of talking to a counselor, an accountability partner, a church leader, or seeking God and finding healing and strength through Him, you quickly jump into another relationship the very first chance you get. Now, this new relationship enables you to mask the pain and hurt the last relationship caused and makes you feel good for the moment.

The new person you are dating is totally unaware that they are your rescuer and the answer to your hurting, bleeding, wounded heart. This is very unfair to them and to you. You have placed such an unrealistic expectation on them to be perfect in every way. As time goes on, your pain and hurt surface again as you begin to see this new perfect person through the filters and lens of your past relationship.

You start being suspicious of their activity and start playing mind games with them to see if your suspicions are valid. Your attitude and emotions jump all over the map every time they don't answer the phone when you call. Then it happens that the perfect person quickly turns into the evil person from your past that caused you so much pain, and now you are reliving the same relationship all over again. This new person quickly realizes that you have trust issues and they leave you.

This is all very unfair to you as well because you yourself haven't allowed yourself to be emotionally healed and now you are just setting yourself up to repeat the cycle again.

4. Volunteer to help others.

You will be amazed at how helping someone else helps you to take your eyes off of your situation. You always get a sense of fulfillment when you take the time to genuinely help others.

There are always opportunities to help people in your church, community, or neighborhood. This is where you will have to be proactive. Search your church website or the event calendar in your city and find places where you can volunteer and interact with others. Do whatever it takes to avoid being a hermit, and get out and meet people while helping others at the same time.

This also puts you in a place to get noticed. You just never know, there could be someone special at a place you are volunteering.

Wil and Angel

Here's a story of how volunteering at your church or in your community can lead to happiness.

Wil and Angel were going to different churches and had never met before. They were both believing in God for that special someone. Ironically, they both were involved in their church outreach group that participated in the same city outreach program for the homeless in the community.

They both had a passion to serve and help others and that's what they did every week. They met each other at the outreach one week and started serving together. They are now happily married and loving every minute of it.

GOD GAVE YOU COMMON SENSE. SO, USE IT.

Being Spiritual Doesn't Mean Being Oblivious

God is a spiritual being, but sometimes we forget that He is very practical. You must learn to not over-spiritualize your dating experience, as it could set you up for disappointment and failure.

Speaking from a guy's perspective and experience in the church arena, many times a single woman is believing in God for a godly man. Ladies, you must first define what that really is and what that really looks like. Is he godly in your eyes just because he goes to church or claps his hands during the song selection in your service? Or is he godly because he serves on the Usher team and greets everyone with a smile and a handshake?

It's important not to idolize his career or the role that he plays at your church. You should still make sure he has those practical qualities that can ensure a healthy relationship.

When I was in Bible school, there were a few times when a girl would tell me that God told her I would be her husband. I'm not saying that God wouldn't do that, but chances are you will scare the person away by saying that because it comes across as just plain weird. Many times in my life, I believe women were more attracted to my position or title than who I was.

Many times in a Christian relationship, people are looking for that special, magical moment in which the heavens split wide open and angels are blowing trumpets, followed by a heavenly bright light that beams down on them with a confirming message that says, "Yes, this is the right one for you." I'm not saying that would never happen but chances are you would be waiting a very long time.

When I met Heather, the thing I liked about her the most was that my title or position was just about the last thing she was interested in. She wanted to get to know me as a person. She had qualities she was looking for in a man, and she wanted to see if I met those qualities. You need to have qualities you are looking for too.

List at least 5 practical qualities that you are looking for in a person:

1. _____
2. _____
3. _____
4. _____
5. _____

Chivalry Is Not Dead

Guys, if you really want to do this God's way then you must step up to the plate and take responsibility for your own actions. It's time to treat women like ladies and, yes, even bring a little chivalry back from the past.

Always remember that a woman's heart is not a play toy, and you shouldn't take it for granted. If you are not into her, then you need to be honest with her and let her know. If you have no intentions of seeing if the relationship could lead to a future marriage and she does, then you need to get out of the way of her meeting her future husband.

I've been in situations where I didn't want to tell a girl that I didn't feel the same way about her because I didn't want to hurt her. In my attempt to keep her heart from being broken, it only made things worse as time went on and eventually she was hurt anyway. Why? Because, although my intentions were good in my own eyes, in all actuality, I was only leading her on.

On the other hand, if you are into her and she is into you, then strive to walk out the relationship in a Godly manner and be the best man that you can be. Keep in mind that she is God's daughter and must be treated with the utmost respect.

Not a Good Fit? Don't Ignore the Feeling

Sometimes you know the right answer before you even ask the question. We have all been in a relationship with the wrong person at one time or another. It started out great only to take a turn for the worse within a month or two. You thought they were the person for you and somehow they turned out to be someone you wished you'd never gotten involved with. More often than not, this could have been so different if you would have paid attention to the feelings you overlooked.

Many times, you can look back over your mistakes and realize you had that funny gut feeling about the person and ignored it only to find yourself in a nightmare, filled with regret. That gut feeling, deep down inside you, is something that directs you and can even warn you at times. You can't explain it and sometimes it just doesn't even make sense. But it's there for a reason. Listening to your feelings can save you from something that you will later on regret.

If the person you're dating is making you better, keep moving forward. If they are making you frustrated, then a goodbye will bring relief.

Don't Date with Blinders On

I (Heather) admit that watching *The Bachelorette* is my guilty pleasure. However, I assure you that my experience and advice does not come from that show.

The show is so unrealistic. Let's face it; you most likely won't be going on romantic dates halfway around the world.

In one season, Desiree was on a mission to find love. Throughout the entire season of her show, she talked about how she had never had a man love her back the way she loved him. She also admitted that the last guy she dated couldn't express his feelings. Yet, on the show, she fell for the only guy who didn't love her back and couldn't express his feelings!

She still couldn't see it because she was dating with blinders on. She had two other men actually say the words "I love you" to her. One of them even expressed his feeling through writing her poetry.

Lucky for her, the guy who wasn't in love with her was honest with her and the show. It wasn't until then that her eyes were opened to the guy who loved her all along.

Why do we want what we can't have or chase after something that will never be ours? Sometimes the best things for us are right in front of us.

YOU'RE READY TO MINGLE!

Congratulations, you are now a dating pro! Hopefully, you've been able to relate to some of the stories we shared and can pull from our advice in future dating situations.

Keep in mind that dating should be fun! Enjoy getting to know someone even if it doesn't go beyond a first or second date. Every date is experience. Take that experience, learn from it, and grow.

If you are struggling to find dates, know that God has a plan for your future. That's right, your future! If you are sitting on the sidelines, it's time to get up, use the equipment we've given you, and get in the game.

If you stumble, get back up again. Do not give up! There is someone out there for you. And always remember to be yourself. You are great at being you and you want that potential person to like you for who you are. So, remember:

1. Dating should be fun.

2. God has a plan for each person's future.

3. Be respectful, honest, and open to communication.

4. Be yourself.

5. Don't give up!

ABOUT THE AUTHORS

Adonis Lenzy

Adonis is a Pastor, Speaker, and Communicator who has a passion to inspire others to live the lives they have imagined. With over twenty years of ministry experience, he truly enjoys encouraging others. He's from San Antonio, Texas, and is a die-hard Dallas Cowboys fan. He also believes that nothing is more important than family. He loves spending time with his wife Heather and two children, Grayson and Kherington. He enjoys playing golf, eating BBQ, and drinking southern-style sweet tea.

Heather Lenzy

Heather is a wife, mother, and a Forensic Scientist. She is from Wisconsin and is a die-hard Green Bay Packers fan! She enjoys quality time with family and friends, baking, golfing, giving relationship advice and has never met a dessert she doesn't like.